Springer Series on **Behavior Therapy and Behavioral Medicine**

Series Editor: Cyril M. Franks, Ph.D.

Advisory Board: John Paul Brady, M.D., Robert P. Liberman, M.D., Neal E. Miller, Ph.D., and Stanley Rachman, Ph.D.

Series volumes no longer in print are listed on the following page.

1986 **Problem-Solving Therapy:** A Social Competence Approach to Clinical Intervention *T. J. D'Zurilla*

1988 **The Psychological Management of Chronic Pain:** A Treatment Manual *H. C. Philips*

1988 **Paradigms in Behavior Therapy:** Present and Promise *D. B. Fishman, F. Rotgers, and C. M. Franks, editors*

1989 **Innovations in Child Behavior Therapy** *M. Hersen, Ph.D., editor*

1990 **Adolescent Behavior Therapy** *E. L. Feindler and G. R. Kalfus, editors*

1990 **Unifying Behavior Therapy:** Contributions of Paradigmatic Behaviorism *G. Eifert and I. Evans, editors*

1990 **Learned Resourcefulness:** On Coping Skills, Self-Control and Adaptive Behavior *M. Rosenbaum, editor*

1990 **Aversive and Nonaversive Interventions:** Controlling Life-Threatening Behavior by the Developmentally Disabled *S. L. Harris and J. S. Handleman, editors*

1992 **Anxiety Across the Lifespan:** A Developmental Perspective *C. G. Last, editor*

1993 **Promoting Health and Mental Health in Children, Youth, and Families** *D. S. Glenwick and L. A. Jason, editors*

1994 **Behavior Therapy in Psychiatric Hospitals** *P. W. Corrigan and R. P. Liberman, editors*

1996 **The Psychological Management of Chronic Pain:** A Treatment Manual—Second Edition *H. Clare Philips and Stanley Rachman* (Accompanying *Patient's Manual* available.)

1996 **Behavior and Personality:** Psychological Behaviorism *Arthur W. Staats*

1997 **Brief but Comprehensive Psychotherapy:** The Multimodal Way *Arnold A. Lazarus*

1976　**Multimodal Behavior Therapy**　*A. A. Lazarus*

1976　**Behavior Therapy Assessment**　*E. J. Mash and L. G. Terdal, editors*

1977　**Behavioral Approaches to Weight Control**　*E. E. Abramson, editor*

1978　**A Practical Guide to Behavioral Assessment**　*Frances J. O'Keefe, Steven A. Kopel, and Steven B. Gordon*

1979　**Asthma Therapy:** A Behavioral Health Care System for Respiratory Disorders　*T. L. Creer*

1980　**Behavioral Medicine:** Practical Applications in Health Care　*B. G. Melamed and L. J. Siegel*

1982　**Multimodal Handbook for a Mental Hospital:** Designing Specific Treatments for Specific Problems　*L. F. Brunell and W. T. Young, editors*

1983　**Eating and Weight Disorders:** Advances in Treatment and Research　*R. K. Goldstein, editor*

1983　**Perspectives on Behavior Therapy in the Eighties**　*M. Rosenbaum, C. M. Franks, and Y. Jaffe, editors*

1983　**Pediatric and Adolescent Behavioral Medicine:** Issues in Treatment　*P. J. McGrath and P. Firestone, editors*

1983　**Hypnosis and Behavior Therapy:** The Treatment of Anxiety and Phobias　*J. C. Clarke and J. A. Jackson*

1984　**Child Obesity:** A New Frontier of Behavior Therapy　*M. D. LeBow*

1983　**Punishment and Its Alternatives:** A New Perspective for Behavior Modification　*J. L. Matson and T. M. DiLorenzo*

1984　**The Binge-Purge Syndrome:** Diagnosis, Treatment, and Research　*R. C. Hawkins, II, W. J. Fremouw, and P. F. Clement, editors*

1985　**Behavioral Assessment in Behavioral Medicine**　*W. W. Tryon, editor*

1985　**Behavior Therapy Casebook**　*M. Hersen and C. Last, editors*

1986　**The Covert Conditioning Handbook**　*J. R. Cautela and A. J. Kearney*

Brief But Comprehensive Psychotherapy

The Multimodal Way

Arnold A. Lazarus,
PhD, ABPP

 Springer Publishing Company

Copyright © 1997 by Springer Publishing Company, Inc.

Springer Publishing Company, Inc.
536 Broadway
New York, NY 10012-3955

Cover design by: Margaret Dunin
Production Editor: Susan Gamer

97 98 99 00 01/5 4 3 2 1

Library of Congress Cataloging-in-Publication Data

Lazarus, Arnold A.
    Brief but comprehensive psychotherapy: the multimodal way /
Arnold A. Lazarus.
        p.   cm.—(Springer series on behavior therapy and behavioral
medicine)
    Includes bibliographical references and index.
    ISBN 0-8261-9640-3
    1. Multimodal psychotherapy.   2. Brief psychotherapy.   I. Title.
II. Series: Springer series on behavior therapy and behavioral
medicine (Unnumbered)
RC489.M84L387   1997
616.89'14—dc21   96-39552
                                                         CIP

Printed in the United States of America

*Read not to contradict and confute, nor to believe and take for granted,
nor to find talk and discourse, but to weigh and consider.*
—Francis Bacon

*Language molds our thoughts; it gives color and shape to our desires; it limits or
extends our sympathies; it gives continuity to our individual self along one line or
another. These effects occur whether we are conscious of them or not.*
—Jacques Barzun

**Arnold A. Lazarus, PhD, ABPP**, is a Fellow of the Academy of Clinical Psychology and holds the rank of Distinguished Professor of Psychology at Rutgers University, where he teaches in the Graduate School of Applied and Professional Psychology. Previously, he served on the faculties of Stanford University, Temple University Medical School, and Yale University. He is a former president of several professional associations and societies and has received many honors and awards for his contributions to clinical theory and therapy, including the Distinguished Psychologist Award from APA's Division of Psychotherapy and the Distinguished Service Award from the American Board of Professional Psychology. Dr. Lazarus is the first recipient (1996) of the prestigious Annual Cummings PSYCHE Award for his innovative and enduring contributions to time-effective psychotherapy. He was inducted as a charter member into the National Academies of Practice as a Distinguished Practitioner in Psychology. In addition to his academic and scholarly activities, he has maintained an active psychotherapy practice since 1959. With sixteen books and over 200 professional and scientific articles to his credit, Dr. Lazarus is widely recognized as an international authority on effective and efficient psychotherapy. He serves on the editorial boards of twelve scientific journals and has given innumberable talks and workshops in the United States and abroad.

Contents

Foreword by Cyril M. Franks   ix

Preface   xiii

1   Let's Cut to the Chase   1

2   Elucidating the Main Rationale   16

3   What Is the Multimodal Way?   25

4   Theories and Techniques   35

5   Multimodal Assessment Procedures:
    Bridging and Tracking   46

6   Multimodal Assessment Procedures:
    Second-Order BASIC I.D. and Structural Profiles   57

7   Some Elements of Effective Brevity   62

8   Activity and Serendipity   71

9   Two Specific Applications:
    Sexual Desire Disorders and Dysthymia   78

10 Couples Therapy   101

11 Some Common Time Wasters   115

Epilogue   123

Appendix 1: Multimodal Life History Inventory   127

Appendix 2: Structural Profile Inventory   143

Appendix 3: Expanded Structural Profile   145

Appendix 4: Marital Satisfaction Questionnaire (Revised)   149

Appendix 5: Article on Eclecticism and Integration (1995)   151

References   165

Author Index   171

Subject Index   175

Foreword

"To heal psychic ailments that we have contracted through misfortunes
or faults of our own, understanding avails nothing,
reasoning little, time much, but resolute action everything."
—*Goethe*

Arnold Lazarus and I have been friends for three decades. We have
shared an office refrigerator; walked and talked together; seen our children
grow up, marry, and remarry; and engaged in numerous heated intellectual
debates. Those who know us primarily through our publications
feel certain that our frequent "few holds barred" written interchanges must
mean that we are bitter enemies. Far from it. Lazarus is a professional colleague
whose companionship I appreciate very much. But none of these
circumstances is the reason why I am glad to write this Foreword. It is my
respect for his accomplishments that motivates me.

According to Mario Puzo, whose sagas of the Sicilian Mafia are in fashion
once again, a "man with a belly" is someone to be reckoned with—
imposing, weighty, and important; a man of substance who has made his
mark on the world for all to see and acknowledge. And so it is with behavior
therapy, argued the late, sorely missed Perry London. Behavior therapy
has grown a belly and become influential and important in its own
right. The questions now before us are: Have Arnold Lazarus and multimodal
therapy achieved a similar status, and is a foreword an appropriate
place to voice this concern? Virtually all mental health professionals would
respond with a resounding "Yes" to the first part of this question, but many

ix

would insist that a foreword is no place to engage in objective and perhaps critical assessments of either multimodal therapy or the professional contribution of Lazarus. A foreword, some would contend, should reflect unqualified endorsement.

My position is clear and unambiguous. Respect for Lazarus and his accomplishments mandates positive but thoughtful consideration of both the man as a professional and his work. While being appropriately supportive, no honest foreword should consist of unrelieved sycophancy. If, as I firmly believe, multimodal therapy—not Lazarus—has indeed grown a belly, a foreword should be the place to put this matter into perspective and, hopefully, conclude on a positive note.

At least for the foreseeable future, for better or worse, managed care is here to stay, and multimodal therapy has to be measured by this yardstick, among other criteria. Not unreasonably, managed care demands demonstrably effective interventions that are valid, short-term, of minimal cost, and consumer-friendly. Most procedures subsumed under the broad umbrella of behavior therapy would seem to meet these criteria. Can the same be said about multimodal therapy? And how, if at all, does multimodal therapy fit into the overall configuration of behavior therapy?

The preface to this book begins by asking if there is any need for, or any room for, yet another book on brief psychotherapy. Lazarus's answer is a decided "Yes," provided that the procedures described are brief, comprehensive, and valid and have not appeared in book form elsewhere. The rest of his text offers a detailed elaboration of multimodal therapy and the manner in which it satisfies these demanding criteria. Multimodal therapy, Lazarus persuasively argues, emphasizes efficiency as well as efficacy and effective coping responses rather than nebulous "cures" of putative deep-seated emotional problems of questionable authenticity. As to the apparent contradiction between the notions of "brief" and "comprehensive," the point is correctly made that it is possible to be brief *and* comprehensive at the same time—provided that the BASIC I.D. spectrum which forms the core of multimodal therapy is fully and conscientiously covered by a clinician trained and versed in its application.

To shed further light on such matters, the reader might wish to think about four pivotal issues as he or she works through this text. Phrased as questions, these are:

1. In theoretical terms, is multimodal therapy a coherent new theoretical model that presents radically different concepts?

2. Is multimodal therapy a significant methodological innovation? If so, what are its specific strengths?
3. Is multimodal therapy really multimodal behavior therapy, and as such, part of mainstream behavior therapy? Or is it something "beyond" behavior therapy, as Lazarus declares here and in his earlier writings?
4. To what extent does brief multimodal therapy meet the needs of managed care, as outlined above? Is it likely to appeal to both practitioners and managed-care administrators?

Now to develop some closure. With regard to question 1, it is my impression, based on a more than cursory knowledge over the years of both behavior therapy and multimodal therapy, that multimodal therapy offers no new theory or postulates. It is and always has been based firmly and consistently upon social learning theory and other concepts of behavior therapy. As such, it is sensitive to new developments and evolving horizons within behavior therapy, which then become incorporated into the core of multimodal therapy, the BASIC I.D. The interesting thing is that Arnold Lazarus himself has made this very point upon many occasions and makes no claim to any new theory.

It is the second question which is of much greater significance and certainly matters most to clinicians. The BASIC I.D. and its derivatives offer an unparalleled system of assessment and intervention that, to the best of my knowledge, has no equal. It is a unique compendium of procedures and therapeutic strategies. If conscientiously and systematically applied, the BASIC I.D. covers the seven key modalities that, individually and interactively, determine how we move, feel, sense, imagine, think, and relate to others. While allowing for creativity and initiative on the part of the clinician, the methodology is most effective if applied systematically, with the precise sequence and format depending on the needs of the situation. Recognizing that, fundamentally, we are all biochemical-neurophysiological entities, Lazarus's "D" modality stands for far more than "drugs." It covers the entire matrix of medical and biological determinants of life itself—including nutrition, exercise, prescribed medications, illicit drugs, tobacco, and legal stimulants and depressants such as caffeine and alcohol. Most important, Lazarus offers a cost-effective system which is eminently teachable and free of mystique or unnecessary jargon. In sum, multimodal therapy stands alone as a methodological tour de force in the annals of assessment and intervention.

The third question is more equivocal, and it is here that Lazarus and I seem to be in disagreement. Conceptualized as "behavior therapy and beyond," Lazarus's system evolved into multimodal behavior therapy. Then it became multimodal therapy. But as far as I am concerned—and I suspect that many behavior therapists would concur—for the reasons elaborated above multimodal therapy is best regarded as behavior therapy in one of its most methodologically sophisticated expressions to date.

Arnold Lazarus practices outstanding behavior therapy but does not call it that. He might consider returning multimodal therapy to the behavior therapy camp where it belongs, thereby acknowledging both his heritage and his seminal contribution to behavior therapy. I make this point primarily to reaffirm my conviction that Lazarus should put the "behavior" back into multimodal therapy.

All of this is minor, so to speak. What really matters is the contribution of Lazarus to the practice of psychotherapy and the unrivaled compatibility of brief multimodal therapy with the goals and aspirations of managed care. Brief multimodal therapy is behavior therapy in one of its most advanced forms. It is efficient, effective, teachable, demonstrably valid, and comprehensive without being rigid. Regardless of the name given to his system, Lazarus has probably contributed more to the clinical needs of individual practitioners and managed-care administrators than anyone else I can think of. Arnold Lazarus, a seasoned campaigner and man for most seasons, if not all, has earned his acknowledged position of leadership in the saga of psychotherapy. It has been a pleasure to write this foreword.

Cyril M. Franks
Distinguished Professor Emeritus
Rutgers University

Preface

Is there a need or any room for yet another book on brief psychotherapy? Yes, but only if it offers strategies and notions that do not appear in the many other tomes, monographs, reports, texts, edited handbooks, manuals, dissertations, and discourses on the subject. The current health care environment has spawned an extensive number of books on short-term, time-limited, cost-effective, and brief forms of psychotherapy. The foregoing terms are not synonomous, but they seem to have two basic features in common. They emphasize efficiency as well as efficacy and usually accentuate the virtues of effective *coping responses* rather than deep-seated emotional "cures." Their central message is "don't waste time."

How can one be *brief* and also *comprehensive?* Is this not a contradiction in terms? Not if one covers what is termed the "BASIC I.D. spectrum"—a concept that is spelled out in chapters 1 and 3 and is amplified in other parts of the book.

Major factors that have made brevity possible in psychotherapy are the learning-based, problem-focused, and solution-oriented approaches, and the evolution of sophisticated and effective techniques for biological assessment and intervention. Whereas many clinicians derided behavior therapists for their emphasis on being active, giving homework assignments, and maintaining specific foci, procedures of this kind have now become standard fare across a diverse range of brief therapies. The present book employs and transcends the customary methods of diagnosis and treatment by providing several unique assessment procedures, as well as many distinctive therapeutic recommendations. It is my opinion that several uncommon ideas are expressed herein that can potentially augment and enhance many readers' skills and clinical repertoires.

I decided not to impose on any of my relatives, friends, or colleagues by asking for advice or reviews of my initial draft, but Dr. Jeffrey A. Rudolph, a former student and now a close friend and esteemed colleague, insisted on reading the entire manuscript. His incisive comments enabled me to clarify and amplify many issues that might otherwise have been downplayed, and I am indeed most grateful to him. I might also mention that it is a privilege and a joy to work with Dr. Ursula Springer and her efficient yet compassionate team.

Arnold A. Lazarus

CHAPTER 1

Let's Cut to the Chase

Anyone can offer brief therapy, but is it possible to provide a course of short-term but comprehensive psychotherapy? My explicit answer is "Often, yes." In the next few pages I will outline exactly how this can be achieved.

BASIC I.D.

At base, we are biological organisms (neurophysiological-biochemical entities) who (1) *behave* (act and react), (2) *emote* (experience affective responses), (3) *sense* (respond to tactile, olfactory, gustatory, visual, and auditory stimuli), (4) *imagine* (conjure up sights, sounds, and other events in our mind's eye), (5) *think* (entertain beliefs, opinions, values, and attitudes), and (6) *interact* with one another (enjoy, tolerate, or suffer various interpersonal relationships). By referring to these six discrete but interactive dimensions or modalities as **B**ehavior, **A**ffect, **S**ensation, **I**magery, **C**ognition, and **I**nterpersonal, and adding a seventh—(7) **D**rugs-Biology—the convenient acronym BASIC I.D. emerges from the initial letters.

Many psychotherapeutic approaches are trimodal, addressing affect, behavior, and cognition—ABC. The multimodal approach provides clinicians with a comprehensive template that permits them to pinpoint salient problems that call for correction. By separating sensations from emotions, distinguishing between images and cognitions, emphasizing both intra-individual and interpersonal behaviors, and underscoring the biological substrate, the multimodal orientation is most far-reaching. By assessing a client's BASIC I.D. one endeavors to "leave no stone unturned."

1

The elements of a rapid yet thorough assessment involve the following range of questions:

B: *Behavior.* What is this individual doing that is getting in the way of his or her happiness or personal fulfillment (self-defeating actions, maladaptive behaviors)? What does the client need to increase and decrease? What should he or she stop doing and start doing?

A: *Affect.* What emotions (affective reactions) are predominant? Are we dealing with anger, anxiety, depression, or combinations thereof, and to what extent (e.g., irritation versus rage; sadness versus profound melancholy)? What appears to generate these negative affects—certain cognitions, images, interpersonal conflicts? And how does the person respond (behave) when feeling a certain way? It is important to look for interactive processes—what impact do various behaviors have on the person's affect and vice versa? How does this influence each of the other modalities?

S: *Sensation.* Are there specific sensory complaints (e.g., tension, chronic pain, tremors)? What feelings, thoughts, and behaviors are connected to these negative sensations? What positive sensations (e.g., visual, auditory, tactile, olfactory, and gustatory delights) does the person report? This includes the individual as a sensual and sexual being. When called for, the enhancement or cultivation of erotic pleasure is a viable therapeutic goal (Rosen & Leiblum, 1995).

I: *Imagery.* What fantasies and images are predominant? What is the person's "self-image"? Are there specific images of success or failure? Are there negative or intrusive images (e.g., flashbacks to unhappy or traumatic experiences)? And how are these images connected to ongoing cognitions, behaviors, affective reactions, etc.?

C: *Cognition.* Can we determine the individual's main attitudes, values, beliefs and opinions? What are this person's predominant shoulds, oughts, and musts? Are there any definite dysfunctional beliefs or irrational ideas? Can we detect any untoward automatic thoughts that undermine his or her functioning?

I.:   *Interpersonal.* Interpersonally, who are the significant others in this individual's life? What does he or she want, desire, expect, and receive from them; and what does he or she, in turn, give to them and do for them? What relationships give him or her particular pleasure and pain?

D.:   *Drugs/biology.* Is this person biologically healthy and health-conscious? Does he or she have any medical complaints or concerns? What relevant details pertain to diet, weight, sleep, exercise, and use of alcohol and drugs?

A more comprehensive problem identification sequence is derived from asking most clients to complete the Multimodal Life History Inventory (Lazarus & Lazarus, 1991). This 15-page questionnaire (see Appendix 1) facilitates treatment by:

- Encouraging clients to focus on specific problems, their sources and attempted solutions;
- Providing focal antecedents, presenting problems, and relevant historical data;
- Generating a valuable perspective regarding a client's style and treatment expectations.

This questionnaire is given to clients as a homework assignment, usually after the initial session. Seriously disturbed (e.g., deluded, deeply depressed, highly agitated) clients will obviously not be expected to comply, but most psychiatric outpatients who are reasonably literate will find the exercise useful for speeding up routine history taking, readily providing the therapist with a BASIC I.D. analysis, and generating a viable treatment plan.

PLACING THE BASIC I.D. IN PERSPECTIVE

In multimodal assessment, the BASIC I.D. serves to remind us to examine each of the seven modalities and their interactive effects. It implies that we are social beings who move, feel, sense, imagine, and think, and that at base we are biochemical-neurophysiological entities. Students and colleagues frequently ask whether any particular areas are more significant, more heavily weighted, than the others. For thoroughness, all seven require careful attention, but perhaps the biological and interpersonal modalities are especially significant.

The biological modality wields a profound influence over all the other modalities. Unpleasant sensory reactions can signal a host of medical illnesses; excessive emotional reactions (anxiety, depression, and rage) may all have biological determinants; faulty thinking and images of gloom, doom, and terror may derive entirely from chemical imbalances; and untoward personal and interpersonal behaviors may stem from many somatic reactions ranging from toxins (e.g., drugs or alcohol) to intracranial lesions. Hence, when any doubts arise about the probable involvement of biological factors, it is imperative to have them fully investigated. A person who has no untoward medical or physical problems and enjoys warm, meaningful, and loving relationships, is apt to find life personally and interpersonally fulfilling. Hence the biological modality serves as the base, and the interpersonal modality is perhaps the apex. The seven modalities are by no means static or linear but exist in a state of reciprocal transaction.

A patient requesting therapy may point to any of the seven modalities as his or her entry point. Affect: "I suffer from anxiety and depression." Behavior: "It's my compulsive habits that are getting to me." Interpersonal: "My wife and I are not getting along." Sensory: "I have these tension headaches and pains in my jaw." Imagery: "I can't get the picture of my grandmother's funeral out of my mind, and I often have disturbing dreams." Cognitive: "I know I set unrealistic goals for myself and expect too much from others, but I can't seem to help it." Biological: "I'm fine as long as I take lithium, but I need someone to monitor my blood levels."

It is more usual, however, for people to enter therapy with explicit problems in two or more modalities—"I have all sorts of aches and pains that my doctor tells me are due to tension. I also worry too much, and I feel frustrated a lot of the time. And I'm very angry with my father." Initially, it is usually advisable to engage the patient by focusing on the issues, modalities, or areas of concern that he or she presents. To deflect the emphasis too soon onto other matters that may seem more important is likely only to make the patient feel discounted. Once rapport has been established, however, it is usually easy to shift to more significant problems.

THE FORMULA

In the spirit of being concise and succinct, here is my formula for brief but comprehensive psychotherapy. My approach to therapy has been shaped mainly by specific outcome and follow-up findings that I have conducted over the past 40 years:

- *First:* Determine whether there are significant problems in each of the following modalities:
  (1) Behavior
  (2) Affect
  (3) Sensation
  (4) Imagery
  (5) Cognition
  (6) Interpersonal relationships
  (7) Drugs-Biology

- *Second:* In concert with the client, select three or four pivotal problems that require specific attention.
- *Third:* If so indicated, make sure the patient undergoes a physical examination and, if necessary, receives medication or psychotropic drugs.
- *Fourth:* Whenever possible, apply empirically validated methods of treatment to specific problems.

Often, in practice, it is unnecessary to address the entire BASIC I.D. When a significant problem in one modality is successfully modified, a ripple effect may mitigate certain difficulties in other modalities. (Remember that the first letters of each of the modalities provide the convenient acronym BASIC I.D.: B=Behavior, A=Affect, S=Sensation, I=Imagery, C=Cognition, I=Interpersonal, and D=Drugs/Biology.)

If one constructive change is achieved in each dimension of the BASIC I.D., the dynamic and synergistic impact of this sevenfold process tends to have widespread effects. Thus, with many individuals, when a pivotal problem in one modality is successfully modified, a ripple effect may mitigate certain difficulties in other modalities, thereby making it unnecessary to address the entire BASIC I.D.

Again, I must emphasize that while it is clinically convenient to divide the reciprocal interactive flux that typifies actual life events into the seemingly separate dimensions of the BASIC I.D., in actuality we are always confronted by a continuous, recursive, multileveled living process. The BASIC I.D. is not a flat, static, linear representation of human experience. I first called BASIC I.D. assessment and systematic treatments multimodal behavior therapy (Lazarus, 1973, 1976); this was later changed to multimodal therapy (MMT) (Lazarus, 1981, 1989).

In essence the multimodal position embodies the following four principles:

1. Human beings act and interact across the seven modalities of the BASIC I.D.
2. These modalities are connected by complex chains of behavior and other psychophysiological events, and they exist in a state of reciprocal transaction.
3. Accurate evaluation (diagnosis) is served by the systematic assessment of each modality and its interaction with every other.
4. Comprehensive therapy calls for specific correction of significant problems across the BASIC I.D.

The multimodal approach essentially asks: (1) What are the specific and interrelated problems across the BASIC I.D.? (2) Who or what appears to be triggering and maintaining these problems? (3) What seems to be the best way in each individual instance of remedying these problems? (4) Have empirically validated methods of change, or specific treatments of choice, been identified to deal with any of the issues? Answers to the foregoing questions procure a systematic structure that ensures thoroughness and also provides specific methods for identifying idiosyncratic reactions.

The reader who has the inclination to read on will find explicit strategies and the rationale for implementing this multimodal process.

WHAT IS MEANT BY BRIEF PSYCHOTHERAPY?

Does "brief" refer mainly to temporal truncation? Is there a specific methodology that qualifies as "brief therapy"? Are the techniques particularly intensive? Is brevity defined by the scope and focus of problems addressed? Are the goals modest? Is brief therapy better than long-term therapy, or is it simply more practical, though suboptimal? I raise these questions simply to show that brief psychotherapy is ill defined and means different things to different clinicians. Perhaps most would agree that *effective therapy depends far less on the hours you put in than on what you put into those hours.* Cooper (1995) points out that brief therapists do not try to accomplish less; they try to "accomplish more with less"—which places significant demands on the clinician to "make many thoughtful and difficult decisions rapidly without rushing the therapy" (pp. 85–86).

There are several temporal considerations. Apart from how many sessions a client should receive, one might ask how long each meeting should last. "Brief contact therapy" with sessions lasting from 10 to 20 minutes was discussed in the 1960s (Dreiblatt & Weatherly, 1965; Koegler & Cannon, 1966). Hoyt (1989) asks whether Berenbaum's (1969) single 10-hour marathon session is a form of prolonged brief therapy or brief prolonged therapy. Unfortunately, even if a clinician determines that a given client will benefit from 15- to 20-minute sessions, he or she will court disaster by submitting the usual bill to government agencies or managed health care concerns that impose a minimum time mandate.

The interval between sessions is another important temporal consideration. Budman (1994) inquired if 10 sessions over a period of 2 years constitute brief therapy. For whom might six discrete 10-minute sessions on a single day prove more helpful than one continuous 60-minute session? Who should be seen twice daily, thrice weekly, or at intervals up to several months apart?

Budman (1994) emphasizes that "time-effective therapy" should not be based on any predetermined number of sessions. He also points out that there is nothing magical about weekly psychotherapy and that sessions can be spaced according to individual needs. Nevertheless, many brief or short-term therapists adhere to a range of about 6 to 12 sessions. Some are more stringent and define brief therapy as lasting from 1 to 10 sessions. Dryden (1995) sets the figure at 11 sessions. Many years ago, one of the first books I had read on brief therapy (Small, 1971) stated that "the range of session contacts defined as brief psychotherapy extended from one to 217 sessions" (p. 21). Small went on to cite numerous authorities who consider brief therapy to be between 1 and 6 sessions, others who held out for 10 to 24 sessions, and a third group reporting brief treatments averaging around 3 to 36 hours. To reiterate, a confounding variable is that some short-term therapists treat their clients weekly for 50- to 60-minute sessions, whereas others employ brief-contact therapy, seeing clients for 15 to 30 minutes several times a week, or even at various times on the same day. Suffice it to say that I regard brief therapy as falling within a range of 1 to 15 hour-long sessions that may occur in close temporal proximity or extend over many months.

The mind boggles at the vast range of heterogeneous ideas that have been discussed under the heading "brief therapy." Budman's edited tome, *Forms of Brief Therapy* (1981; reissued in 1995), has 17 chapters that cover wide-ranging ideological and technical differences. Similarly, Wells and Gianetti's (1990) edited *Handbook on the Brief Psychotherapies* (1990), and the 490-page book by Zeig and Gilligan *Brief Therapy: Myths, Methods, and Metaphors* (1990) traverse additional territory. Nevertheless, as Budman states in the 1995 update of *Forms of Brief Therapy:* "When therapists are evaluated for participation in managed care networks, one of the first questions asked is, 'Are you trained and experienced as a brief therapist?'" (p.464). In this connection, Hoyt's *Brief Therapy and Managed Care* (1995) may be viewed as a standard reference and vade mecum.

SELECTION CRITERIA

Before discussing the matter further, it is necessary to discuss for whom brief therapy may be suitable or unsuitable. It is obvious that YAVIS (Young, Attractive, Verbal, Intelligent, and Successful) clients are the best candidates for any form of therapy. Some theorists (e.g., Davanloo, 1978; Sifneos, 1992) put forth stringent inclusion criteria while others are not as exacting (e.g., Budman & Gurman, 1988). Two detailed studies—one by Howard, Kopta, Krause, and Orlinsky (1986), and another by Kopta, Howard, Lowry, and Beutler (1994)—showed that 48% to 58% of anxious and depressed clients were measurably improved after eight sessions and 75% to 80% were markedly improved at the end of 6 months (26 sessions). Borderline patients, however, fared less well—only 38% were improved by 26 sessions. People displaying "character symptoms" (e.g., admitting to having urges to harm others, displaying strong mistrust, and holding beliefs about possessing mental abnormalities) often showed little change even after 100 sessions.

From a multimodal standpoint, we have found that clients whose Modality Profiles (see chapter 3) have in excess of two dozen interrelated problems are likely to require more than 15 sessions to derive substantial benefits from treatment. People who may be called "precontemplators" (see Prochaska, Norcross, & DiClemente, 1994) are not suitable candidates for brief therapy—or perhaps for any form of therapy, for that matter. These are individuals who resist change and refuse to acknowledge that they need help. Such folks usually require careful coaxing and elaborate shaping before they become open to meaningful assistance. It is also extremely difficult to work briefly with people who couch their problems in vague terms so that goal setting remains nebulous and confusing. Although some may disagree, I regard as unsuitable for brief therapy chronic substance abusers and clients who reveal a global assessment of everyday functioning of 50 or below on Axis V in *DSM-IV*. Such patients usually have suicidal ideation, show social and occupational impairment, and may at times be incoherent and violent.

All problems are part of a continuum from mild to extreme. Thus, pervasively anxious clients do not appear to be good candidates for brief therapy compared with those so-called "anxiety neurotics" whose fears are less extreme and more circumscribed. Similarly those invasive, high-maintenance borderlines who are characterized by frequent self-mutilation, extreme acting out, undue manipulative tactics, repeated threats, and incessant harassment of their therapists are not suitable candidates for brief therapy. Yet there are many patients diagnosed with borderline personality disorders who can contain their anxiety sufficiently to respect boundaries and who are capable of deriving benefit from 10 to 15 sessions of brief multimodal therapy. It is not so much the diagnostic label that determines whether someone can profit from focused or short-term therapy as much as the *degree of disturbance* or the *extent of emotional disruption*. Thus some clients with a posttraumatic stress disorder or an obsessive-compulsive disorder, or those displaying frequent panic attacks, are good candidates for brief therapy, whereas others are not. On the subject of posttraumatic stress disorder (PTSD), I strongly recommend Meichenbaum's (1994) highly informative manual on the assessment and treatment of PTSD. He provides extensive information for clinicians who want an in-depth understanding of the problems surrounding traumatic events in people's lives.

EIGHT ISSUES

I submit that if a therapist wants to be effective, retain a constructive focus, arrive at creative solutions, and be both short-term and comprehensive, the following eight issues must be ruled out or adequately dealt with, if necessary:

1. Conflicting or ambivalent feelings or reactions
2. Maladaptive behaviors
3. Misinformation (especially dysfunctional beliefs)
4. Missing information (e.g., skill deficits, ignorance, or naiveté)
5. Interpersonal pressures and demands
6. Biological dysfunctions
7. External stressors outside the immediate interpersonal network (e.g., poor living conditions, unsafe environment)
8. Traumatic experiences (e.g., sexual abuse or gross neglect in childhood)

I have rarely treated anyone who did not manifest the first five issues. Everyone is conflicted about something and has at least one or two unfortunate habits. Few things are cut and dried, and ambivalence is ubiquitous. Likewise, we are all misinformed about certain subjects or factors, and to a greater or lesser extent everybody lacks certain skills and significant pieces of information (i.e., is missing information). As for interpersonal pressures and demands, only a hermit can escape these realities, but complete and total social withdrawal is not exactly a healthy solution; therefore, the acquisition of interpersonal proficiency is essential. If biological dysfunctions are present or suspected, the necessary medical attention becomes a high priority.

In my experience, when external stressors or severe traumatic experiences are part of the variance, it is usually necessary to consult outside resources and agencies, and effective or meaningful short-term interventions become less likely. Thus, poverty- stricken individuals will benefit more from social agencies that can help them with welfare and food stamps. Victims of extreme traumatic events usually need social and community support in addition to specific psychotherapeutic interventions.

THE INITIAL INTERVIEW IN BRIEF THERAPY

To remain focused and targeted, the initial interview should try to address each of the following:

1. What were the presenting complaints and their main precipitating events?
2. What seemed to be some significant antecedent factors?
3. Who or what appeared to be maintaining the client's maladaptive behaviors?
4. Was it fairly evident what the client wished to derive from therapy?
5. What are some of the client's strengths or positive attributes?
6. Why is the client seeking therapy at this particular time?
7. What was the client's appearance with respect to physical characteristics, grooming, manner of speaking, and attitude?
8. Were there any signs of "psychosis" (e.g., thought disorders, delusions, incongruity of affect, bizarre or inappropriate behaviors)?
9. Was there evidence of self-recrimination, depression, homicidal or suicidal tendencies?
10. Did it seem that a mutually satisfying relationship could be established, or should the client be referred elsewhere?
11. Were there any indications or contraindications for the adoption of a particular therapeutic pace and style (e.g., cold, warm, formal, informal, supportive, confrontational, tough, or tender)?
12. Did the client emerge with legitimate grounds for hope?

Obviously, an initial interview with someone who is seriously impaired, non-verbal, or extremely withdrawn will not shed light on all the foregoing issues. The implication of the 12 points is that the initial interview not only identifies significant trends, problems, and functional connections but also provides a framework for assessing the timing and cadence of each interaction.

FIVE PREVALENT MYTHS ABOUT PSYCHOTHERAPY

The field of psychotherapy is riddled with myths and superstitions. Here are five that undermine effective short-term therapy:

- *Myth 1:* Depth of therapy is more important than breadth of therapy.
- *Myth 2:* It is all in the relationship.
- *Myth 3:* Changes automatically generalize.

- *Myth 4:* Do not overstep therapeutic boundaries.
- *Myth 5:* Noncompliance with or nonadherence to treatment recommendations is a sign of "resistance."

Each of these myths will now be briefly discussed.

Breadth versus Depth

My follow-ups suggest that if a therapist focuses narrowly on only one dimension, treatment gains will probably not endure. The importance of *breadth* can hardly be overemphasized. Those who emphasize *depth* are apt to probe specific elements of their patients' unconscious processes. Thus, some short-term psychodynamic therapists focus exclusively on preoedipal or oedipal conflicts; others address their clients' separation anxiety or dwell solely on interpersonal role disputes. Certain cognitive therapists attend only to cognitive distortions or irrational beliefs. Such tactics will, from my point of view, overlook significant aspects that call for remediation. I have seen many clients who claimed to have attained profound insights after spending many years in insight-oriented therapy but who still embraced dysfunctional philosophies of life (probably because nobody had specifically disputed their irrational ideas), who were still very tense (partly because they had never learned how to apply straightforward deep muscle relaxation), and who suffered as a result of (sometimes extreme) interpersonal ineptitude (because they had never acquired the necessary social skills).

The Client-Therapist Relationship

Here is a typical (misleading) sentiment: "What the individual therapist *is* rings louder than what he or she *does*" (Goodkin, 1981, p. 6). Of course, the therapist's personality, degree of caring, capacity to communicate, and ability to empathize—and his or her other personal characteristics—are essential, but in and of itself, even the most loving, caring, articulate clinician will not help most obsessive-compulsives, phobics, bipolar depressives, clients with extreme panic disorder, or individuals with specific sexual dysfunctions (to name a few conditions) unless he or she knows how to administer specific treatments of choice. "The therapeutic relationship is the soil that enables the techniques to take root" (Lazarus & Fay, 1984). On occasion, the relationship can provide an adequate degree of facilitation to be both necessary and sufficient (an idea which Rogers, 1957, had posited across the board and which his followers still echo), but in the majority of instances a good working alliance is *usually necessary but often insufficient* (Fay & Lazarus, 1993). In essence, effective therapy calls for appropriate techniques, correctly administered, within the context of a trusting and caring relationship. The relationship serves to educate, motivate, generate, formulate, and separate problems and solutions.

Generalization

It is surprising that many still believe that a change in the consulting room automatically generalizes to the client's everyday life. Recently, a therapist remarked: "When Charlie first joined my group, he was so reticent that he hardly said a word. Within 3 or 4 sessions he became a veritable cotherapist—active and outgoing." I asked: "Have you determined if these gains have extended outside the confines of your particular group?" The therapist replied: "Of course they have." One cannot take this for granted. I know many an individual who became extremely proficient at group therapy but who remained taciturn and uncommunicative in other settings. Homework assignments and various in vivo excursions are frequently necessary to ensure that changes in the office extend into the client's work, home, and social environments. Careful monitoring of between session assignments serves to validate where insight and knowledge has led to performance-based change.

Transcending Boundaries

A considerable literature exists exhorting and warning therapists to be aware of and to respect boundaries. A few of these include such admonitions as: maintain the therapist's neutrality, protect the patient's confidentiality, avoid any personal relationship with patients, obtain informed consent before implementing specific treatments, refrain from physical contact, eschew dual relationships, and minimize self-disclosure by the therapist. The intent behind boundary formulations is to safeguard patients' welfare and to avoid harming, exploiting, or harassing patients. The aim is to ensure that clients are treated with the utmost respect, dignity, and integrity. Nevertheless, as I have underscored (Lazarus, 1994), when taken too far, these well-intentioned guidelines can backfire. Thus, many therapists would never consider discussing matters with a client at a restaurant because they would label that a "dual relationship," they would refuse to accept the simplest of gifts because they insist that the therapist must receive nothing from the client other than the fee for service, and they would decline an invitation to attend a client's wedding on the ground that it can be extremely disadvantageous to venture beyond the private and professional setting (Borys, 1994). At this juncture let it simply be noted that the practice of brief but comprehensive psychotherapy calls for the therapist's willingness to offer more robust methods than pure conversation and to be disposed to take some calculated risks. Differences between boundary violations and boundary crossings is elaborated upon toward the end of chapter 2.

Noncompliance and "Resistance"

Instead of attributing lack of therapeutic progress to the patient's "resistance," it is preferable to ascribe most treatment failures to the limitations of our knowledge and the constraints of our personalities. Treatment impasses are likely to be caused by such factors as inappropriate therapist-client matching, the absence of rapport, the therapist's use of incorrect techniques or faulty application of appropriate procedures, and a failure to properly identify situations that maintain or reinforce the client's problems (Lazarus & Fay, 1982). Therapists who postulate an internal agent—"resistance"—are less likely to look for extrinsic sources that undermine progress.

The most obvious manifestation of noncompliance is a client's failure to carry out an agreed-upon homework assignment. Instead of assuming that some unspecified "resistance" lies behind most instances of nonadherence, it is more profitable to consider a variety of concrete possibilities:

- Was the assignment expressed in sufficient detail and clearly understood?
- Was the assignment irrelevant or not especially pertinent?
- Was it too threatening?
- Was it too time-consuming and not "cost-effective?"
- Was the patient insufficiently schooled regarding the rationale and value of homework assignments?
- Was the patient opposed to self-help ministrations?
- Was the therapeutic relationship strained or faulty?
- Was someone in the patient's network sabotaging the therapy?
- Was the patient receiving too many secondary gains to relinquish his or her maladaptive behaviors?

RELATIONSHIP STYLES

One final point needs to be underscored in this succinct overview. Truly brief but effective therapy will depend on two major factors: (1) the implementation of the correct techniques in the proper manner, and (2) the therapist's ability to be an *authentic chameleon*. It is most important to determine whether the client will respond best to someone who is directive, supportive, reflective, cold, warm, tepid, formal, or informal. The therapist's *style* is as significant as his or her *methods* (Lazarus, 1993). Thus, the essence of cost-effective brief therapy underscores the notion that treatment should be "custom-made" for the client. The client's needs come before the therapist's theoretical framework. Instead of placing clients on a Procrustean bed and treating them alike, multimodal therapists look for a broad but tailor-made panoply of effective techniques to bring to bear upon the problem. The methods are carefully applied within an appropriate context and delivered in a style or manner that is most likely to have a positive impact.

How does the clinician determine specific relationships of choice? By very carefully observing the client's reactions to various statements, tactics, and strategies. One begins neutrally by offering the usual facilitative conditions—the therapist listens attentively, expresses caring and concern, exudes empathy—and notes the client's reactions. If there are clear signs of progress, one offers more of the same; if not, the clinician may take a more active or directive position and note whether this proves effective.

In summary, for a broad-based, focused, and meaningful clinical impact:

1. Traverse the BASIC I.D.
2. Rule out or deal with the eight factors listed on page 9.
3. Endeavor to address 12 issues in the initial interview (see page 10).
4. Avoid five prevalent myths.
5. Determine specific "relationships of choice."

Many people have read the classic little book, *The Elements of Style,* in which E.B. White recounted how William Strunk Jr. waxed eloquent on the beauty of brevity in the use of English:

> *Vigorous writing is concise. A sentence should contain no unnecessary words, a paragraph no unnecessary sentences, for the same reason that a drawing should have no unnecessary lines and a machine no unnecessary parts. This*

requires not that the writer make all his sentences short, or that he avoid all detail and treat his subject only in outline, but that every word tell. (Strunk & White, 1979, p. 23)

Analogizing from the elements of literary style to the fundamentals of brief and effective psychotherapy, I contend that:

Good therapy is precise. A session should contain no unnecessary psychological tests, no protracted or redundant methods, no needless techniques, no prolonged silence, and as little dilatory rhetoric as possible. This requires not that the therapist gloss over important details, nor that he or she forgo thoroughness for the sake of brevity, but that every intervention tell.

The remainder of this book will place each of the foregoing points into perspective and elaborate on numerous other factors and processes that enhance the practice of brief but comprehensive psychotherapy.

CHAPTER 2

Elucidating the Main Rationale

W hen someone comes to you for therapy, how do you typically treat him or her? I posed that question to a well-known psychiatrist. "I'm a family therapist," he replied, "so when patients call to set up an appointment, I try to persuade them to bring as many family members as possible to our first and subsequent sessions."

Another therapist answered the same question as follows: "I don't 'treat' people. Treatment implies a medical model which, to my way of thinking, is misleading. . . . I try to help people understand themselves."

A third clinician said: "I provide a warm, nonjudgmental, and empathic relationship that facilitates emotional openness and growth."

If I were asked this question, I would say that my method of treatment would depend, at the very least, on the needs, context, expectations, personality, and problems of the person asking for help. In some cases, it is highly advisable and much quicker to work with an entire family. In other instances, one-on-one individual therapy is best. Some people profit from a type of therapy that enables them to gain insight and self-understanding; others require a more active training program in interpersonal skills. Some people blossom in an atmosphere of therapeutic warmth and empathy; others prefer a more formal businesslike relationship. In my estimation, we need *bespoke therapy*—methods that are carefully tailored and custom-made. But whatever we do, we can ill afford to waste time!

TWO CASES IN POINT

Consider Maria, a 10-year-old Hispanic girl of Puerto Rican and Domini-
can descent who was described as being noncompliant at home and at
school. She was mildly retarded, with delays in language abilities; had
attention-deficit hyperactivity disorder (ADHD); and was placed on Ritalin,
10 mg, b.i.d., but was often unwilling to take the medication. On those
occasions when she did adhere to the Ritalin regimen, she was reported
to be significantly less hyperactive and distractible, less inclined to fight
with her siblings, and better able to concentrate on her schoolwork. A pre-
liminary assessment suggested that Maria's problematic behaviors would
diminish if her (preliterate) mother—who only spoke Spanish—could
acquire the skills necessary to carry out a positive reinforcement program.

What type of therapy and therapist would be most likely to make head-
way with Maria? How effective would a so-called person-centered therapist
be who offered warmth, empathy, genuineness, and other facilitative conditions to the nth degree? Or how about an insight-oriented therapist?
Would Maria derive significant benefit from greater self-awareness—
notwithstanding her limited IQ? In my estimation, neither one of these
therapists could provide the proper match or the necessary ingredients to
resolve Maria's problems.

The therapist selected to treat this child was Dr. Anna Abenis-Cintron,
at the time an intern in a developmental clinic in the South Bronx. As the
case unfolded, it became clear that the therapist's fluency in Spanish, her
good working knowledge of behavioral principles, and her familiarity with
Hispanic culture, were all essential.

As Dr. Cintron pointed out: "Latinos tend to embrace a high degree of
formality and respect for authority. Professionals must be sensitive to the
Latino's vulnerability to authority. This necessitated that I remain vigilant
regarding overcompliance. The mother could possibly become over-
compliant secondary to her belief that she did not have equal standing
and no right to object to my directives. I had to be cognizant that I was
restricting the choices and manipulating the environment of a voluntary
client who would be less assertive in part owing to her cultural beliefs. I
had to make opportunities available to empower the mother and limit
her dependency."

Although the father was seen on one occasion and was carefully factored
into the therapy, there appeared to be no need for formal "family therapy," and there were strong indications that active involvement of the siblings would have undermined the therapeutic process.

Once again, let us consider if an approach that focused only on self-understanding or insight, or one that dwelled exclusively on a facilitative therapeutic relationship (minus specific skills training), would have achieved very much. I strongly doubt it. The need for an appropriate match between therapist and patient, plus the use of appropriate techniques, cannot be overstated. I will argue throughout this book that therapists who approach their patients with a predetermined or a priori mind-set will, at the very least, fail to help many of the people who consult them. A great many clients who could be helped often derive little benefit at all—simply because the "right therapy" by the appropriate therapist was never administered.

Thus, 40-year-old Don, who was in many ways quite antithetical to 10-year-old Maria, had an interesting agenda and a definite bias regarding the credentials he would consider for anyone worthy of being his therapist. An extremely bright, talented, urbane, articulate, and sophisticated scientist, Don had parlayed his academic credentials into his own lucrative business. He sought help because of an unsuccessful track record with women. Don's failures seemed to stem from little more than an inept interpersonal style due mainly to poor parental modeling and example, and it seemed apparent that he could benefit from a brief and focused regimen of intensive social skills training. But there was a catch. As a biographee in *Who's Who in America,* he insisted that the necessary camaraderie for an effective therapeutic relationship would most likely ensue only if his therapist also appeared in *Who's Who.* This type of elitist thinking betrayed a snobbish and judgmental outlook that called for correction in its own right, but not at the outset of therapy. A compatible match between patient and therapist is often a sine qua non for an effective outcome; at the very least it will enhance the placebo effects.

As already mentioned in chapter 1, effective clinicians need to be "authentic chameleons" (Lazarus, 1993) who can adapt themselves to the expectations of different individuals and situations. But there is a limit; a definite cutoff point of individual expertise obviously exists. The specific list of contents comprised by the *DSM-IV* classification of mental disorders occupies 12 pages of print and cites well over 400 different afflictions. Obviously there is no therapist capable of managing each and every psychiatric disorder. Perhaps the first axiom of effective and efficient therapy is: *"Know your limitations; try to stay in touch with practitioners who possess knowledge and skills that you do not; and don't hesitate to make appropriate referrals."*

FROM UNIMODAL TO MULTIMODAL PERSPECTIVES

During the 1950s and 1960s "unimodal" solutions to mental and emotional suffering were predominant. "Make the unconscious conscious!" "Change maladaptive behaviors!" "Modify faulty cognitions!" Circa 1956, when I was a graduate student working at a treatment center for alcohol abuse in Johannesburg, South Africa, the psychiatrists had two tricks up their sleeve—Antabuse (a chemical that produced unpleasant and potentially dangerous side effects if someone imbibed alcohol while on the medication) and what they called "conditioned reflex therapy" (wherein they gave the patients emetic drugs and then served them alcohol—on the assumption that they would forever associate the violent nausea and vomiting that ensued with the ingestion of alcohol). My displeasure with this bimodal approach resulted in my first professional publication (Lazarus, 1956) in which I reported some studies I had conducted, leading to the following conclusion:

> *The emphasis in the rehabilitation of the alcoholic must essentially be on a* synthesis, *which would embrace active measures combined with educative procedures and psychotherapeutic and socio-economic procedures, as well as innumerable adjunctive measures such as drug therapy, vitamin therapy and the like. (p. 710)*

Thus, the stage was set for the practice of a "broad-spectrum" therapy when treating alcoholics (Lazarus, 1965), or any other disorder (Lazarus, 1969; 1971). The importance of *breadth* without sacrificing *depth* became a primary focus and culminated in the multimodal orientation (Lazarus, 1976, 1989). But in this era of managed health care and other restrictions on prolonged psychotherapy, new issues have arisen. One of the major concerns is whether one can practice brief therapy or short-term therapy without shortchanging the patient. And that is precisely what this book hopes to achieve.

Since its inception, multimodal therapy (MMT) has grown extensively. For example, the methods discussed in chapters 5 and 6 were added and refined and underscore unique assessment procedures employed only by MMT clinicians. Throughout the book, the reader will find numerous examples of tactics and methods that were added to the essential repertoire over the ensuing years. Thus, it is astonishing that Beutler, Consoli, and Williams (1995) referred to the relatively unchanged nature of MMT "since its formulation in 1976" (p. 275). As the reader will discover, the multimodal orientation provides a rich array of methods for achieving rapid and accurate accounts of major problems, their interactive elements, and strategies for selecting treatments of choice. MMT in general and this book in particular fall within the genre which Peterson (1995) calls *education for practice* and which he says "is neither science nor art but a profession in itself" (p. 975).

MORE ABOUT BOUNDARIES

Although the topic of boundaries in psychotherapy is not specific to brief or short-term therapy, it is nevertheless extremely important and can often interfere with the process of effective treatment, thereby undermining timely solutions in many situations. Specific boundaries have been proposed to protect patients from exploitation and any form of harassment and discrimination, and to emphasize the significance of respect, integrity, confidentiality, and informed consent (see *American Psychologist*, 1992, Vol. *47*, No. 12). In many circles these well-intentioned guidelines have reached a point of absurdity and are transformed into rigid straitjackets that force clinicians into a remote and cold posture.

Perhaps the most serious boundary violation occurs when a therapist abandons his or her fiduciary responsibilities by entering into a sexual relationship with a patient. However, some authorities seem to have sex on the brain and regard any and all boundary crossings as a "slippery slope" that will probably culminate in sexual intercourse (e.g., Gabbard & Nadelson, 1995a; Gutheil, 1989, 1994). It may be true that unethical and predatory therapists with sexual intentions in mind might begin to pave the way by scheduling the client at times when nobody else is present, prolonging the therapy sessions, making inappropriate personal revelations, using suggestive language, arranging meetings outside the office, offering services above and beyond the call of duty, contributing gifts, greatly reducing or waiving the fee, and making seemingly innocent physical overtures. Yet in the hands of highly ethical and professional therapists, many of the foregoing actions may facilitate and greatly enhance treatment. Thus, selective self-disclosure, the willingness to see a client at odd times and to run over time, occasional availability outside the confines of the consulting room, and a sliding fee scale may all enhance rapport and augment a positive treatment outcome.

Nonetheless Gabbard and Nadelson (1995b) aver and forewarn that benevolent, honest, ethical, and well-intentioned therapists "are swept away by feelings of love for the patient or neediness for themselves in times of personal stress in their lives" (p. 1346). They imply that only awareness of and resolute adherence to very strict boundaries can offset the tendency for therapists to fall prey to personal agendas. The ardent acceptance of the ubiquitous "slippery slope" notion can only foster such mistrust that clinical judgment would be hindered and the capacity to help many individuals would be undermined. Fay (1995) pointed to the essential error in logic behind the "slippery slope" argument. "Sexual exploitation of patients by physicians is usually preceded by other behaviors (e.g., self-disclosure); therefore, physicians who engage in such non-sexual 'boundary violations' are likely to exploit their patients sexually" (p. 1345).

Let me not be misunderstood. All practitioners should be trained to appreciate the importance of essential boundaries, to fully comprehend what constitute boundary violations, and to understand the potential repercussions therefrom. We must always respect the patient's dignity while protecting him or her from any harm, especially iatrogenic indiscretions. Thus, sexual contact, exploitation of any kind, and the misuse of power differentials should be studiously avoided. A point that is often overlooked is that there is an enormous difference between *violating* boundaries and *transcending* or *crossing* them under certain circumstances.

For example, a therapist was treating an adolescent and wanted to arrange a meeting with the boy's mother, a busy professional. The mother's schedule was such that the most convenient time was during a lunch break, and she suggested they meet to discuss the matter at a local restaurant. To dine with a client in a restaurant would be seen by many as a dual relationship and hence as a boundary transgression. Indeed, if the therapist, for instance, suspected that the mother had romantic intentions in mind, I would recommend that meetings be confined to the professional setting. However, if there are no a priori reasons to suspect ulterior motives, why not expedite matters by discussing the boy at any mutually convenient location—be it at the mother's place of work, in a hotel lobby, in a park, or elsewhere? Should unforeseen difficulties arise, these can become grist for the mill and appropriately managed. Incidentally, I would typically not be the one to suggest this boundary crossing. Some clients would be mortified at the thought of being seen in public with a therapist. But if the client makes the suggestion, the pros and cons can rapidly be considered and acted upon.

What exactly is a dual relationship? Are all dual relationships inherently inimical to successful therapy? Clients or therapists who develop a joint business venture while therapy is ongoing are obviously engaging in a dual relationship. To my mind, this could prove positive, neutral, or negative depending on individual circumstances, but it is a practice that I would strongly caution against because there seem to be too many potential downsides.

In a different context, I have had the opportunity to read books on business management aimed at company presidents and middle managers who are interested in successful organizational change. These books discuss their authors' commitment to devising a better way of transacting business, of dealing with employees, and of aiming at more appropriate targets. They nearly all refer to the courage to challenge existing norms and power bases. The recommendations of these entrepreneurs and company consultants, and the suggestions offered by many short-term, action-oriented psychotherapists, are remarkably similar. I was particularly struck by Katzenbach, who, in his book *Real Change Leaders* (1995), discussed the personal initiative to go beyond defined boundaries, to break bottlenecks, challenge the status quo, and think outside the box. Truly effective therapists, like Katzenbach's RCLs (real change leaders), are not frightened conformists but courageous and enterprising helpers, willing to take calculated risks.

Some years ago, while reading a book on psychodrama by Kellermann (1992), I was particularly impressed with his account of a client who had been treated by Zerka Moreno, one of the cofounders of psychodrama. When asked what she had found most helpful, the client stated:

> *The most important things for me was that I established a close relationship with Zerka, a kind of friendship which extended beyond the ordinary patient-therapist relation. She took me to restaurants and on trips and treated me like my own mother had never done. That friendship had such a great impact on me that I can feel its effects to this very day! (p. 133)*

What is to be inferred from this revelation? That all our clients should be taken to restaurants and on trips? Hardly! The point is whether or not the therapist is willing and able to cross certain boundaries in those rare instances where it seems likely that salubrious results will ensue. As I have underscored elsewhere (Lazarus, 1995), it is usually inadvisable to disregard strict boundary limits in the presence of severe psychopathology. This goes beyond frank psychoses and includes anyone with passive-aggressive, antisocial, histrionic, paranoid, narcissistic, schizoid, or borderline personality features. In such cases very strict adherence to delimited boundaries is strongly advised. But those practitioners (and, regrettably, they are not few or far between) who impose rigid limits across the board will fail to help people who might otherwise have benefited from their ministrations.

For example, one of my clients, a financially successful stockbroker who came for treatment because of an extreme penchant toward self-criticism and problems with self-confidence had worked with me for about 3 months and improved considerably. Toward the end of a session he said, "Would you and your wife come to our home for dinner?" In terms of response-couplets, clinicians have milliseconds to decide how best to react to most statements from clients. Immediately, I felt that this was a test. If I hesitated, he'd feel demeaned and disconfirmed. In his case, I sensed that the metacommunication behind his invitation was: "Let's see if the foundation upon which we have built our entire therapeutic relationship is genuine. You have stressed parity as a philosophy of life and have stated that I am your peer. Thus, unless you have inviolate grounds for declining my invitation, your nonacceptance will make a mockery out of everything you have averred." Had I said, "Let's discuss this when the therapy has ended," he would probably have read far more than personal rejection into it, and would have concluded, probably irrevocably, that I had lied to him. Immediately I simply said, "I can't speak for my wife, but I'd be honored." We duly dined at their home, met some good friends of theirs who knew the situation, and a pleasant evening ensued. A couple of months later, as a matter of social propriety, the client and his wife were dinner guests at our home. This temporary "dual relationship" provided the client with the affirmation he desired. It is my strong impression that had I gone by the book and refused to enter into these social exchanges, his therapeutic gains may have been overturned.

How often have I accepted dinner invitation from clients? In some 40 years of practice, I doubt if the number exceeds half a dozen. In perfect candor, there have been many clients with whom any form of socialization, even if not clinically contraindicated, would have constituted tedious work. One can usually manage to deal constructively with their feelings of rejection when such invitations are graciously declined. The foregoing case, however, given the terrain we had traversed, was an exception.

Too many therapists seem to have as their raison d'être a need to see themselves as extraordinarily powerful healers. Consequently, they tend to infantilize and overpathologize their patients, viewing them as extremely fragile. A chapter by Anderson (1992) is a striking example. He portrays all psychotherapy clients as veritable infants, incapable of making autonomous or mature decisions, and quite unfit to establish consensual relationships. Few clinicians are as extreme as Anderson, but their range of proscriptions is nevertheless vast. For example, they studiously avoid disclosing any personal information; they refuse to accept even token gifts from clients; they eschew any response that would seem informal or casual rather than strictly professional; and they champion various other absolutistic injunctions predicated on the notion that it is *never* acceptable to receive anything from a client other than the agreed-upon fee for service. I draw these conclusions mainly from what my supervisees tell me about their other supervisors. It is significant that Milton H. Erickson, arguably one of the most creative and effective therapists of our time, constantly disregarded other people's proscriptions—"he would do a home visit . . . take somebody to a restaurant, as well as work in his office" (Haley, 1993, p. 88). Many therapists will be appalled to learn that Erickson's waiting room was his home living room, where his young children frolicked while his patients waited. "And to think that his kids were in there playing with his patients, some of whom he described as really rather far-out people . . . [with] the dog barking outside, and his wife hollering for the children" (Haley, 1993, pp. 82–83).

It seems to me that boundary crossings should be determined on an individualistic basis. Whenever a therapist who is about to cross a boundary feels it necessary to examine his or her own motives and calculate the pros and cons, it is probably best to refrain from the intended venture. Thus, I was about to ask a client if he'd mind collecting my restrung tennis racquet from a store right next door to his own place of work. I hesitated and thought it through more clearly. He would probably see it as exploitation on my part, although he was not being asked to go out of his way. I could envision him feeling that I was using him as a delivery boy. Consequently, I dispensed with the idea and drove the 14 mile round-trip to pick up my racquet. With someone else, I may not have hesitated to say, "Hey, Charlie, would you be a pal and pick up my racquet from the tennis shop for me?" knowing full well that he'd be delighted to do me that small favor.

It has been argued that competent therapists are apt to use clinical judgment rather than rely on a cookbook approach in providing services to their clients. Nevertheless, less experienced practitioners, or those whose judgment is perhaps somewhat questionable, are best advised to adhere to all recognized boundary prohibitions. But if a client has the decency to pick up a hot beverage for you on a cold winter's day, have the courtesy to accept it graciously—unless you strongly suspect that it has been laced with poison!

CHAPTER 3

What Is the Multimodal Way?

Some of the issues that were hotly debated when I was a student more than 40 years ago have faded into oblivion. Others are still very much with us, and a few have been revised or modified. For example, as an undergraduate I learned that psychology is the "science of behavior" and that whatever we know or can infer about a person comes solely from his or her actions or conduct. There is, of course, a lot of truth to this. How can we know what somebody is feeling? By the way she or he acts. "Look how uptight Charleen is—her hands are shaking, she is trembling all over and appears to be drenched with perspiration!" "Bobby seems so depressed— his eyes are downcast, he can't get going, he never smiles, and he is often on the verge of tears." Or people can verbalize (provide information about) their feelings—another form of behavior. "I am feeling very discouraged about the future—all I can picture are images that spell trouble ahead." Measuring instruments can sometimes pick up involuntary behaviors that reveal a person's emotions (e.g., the use of polygraphs).

It was not uncommon between 1950 and 1970 to hear the following sentiment: "If you can't observe it or measure it, it probably doesn't exist!" During that period, many of my behavioral colleagues pretty much glossed over thoughts, feelings, attitudes, opinions, values, images, and beliefs, dismissing them simply as a subset of different forms of covert behavior. Indeed, in some circles, inserting the word "behavior" after any description, was considered to make the result more measurable and thus more scientific. We no longer ate but engaged in "eating behaviors"; we didn't think but performed "thinking behaviors," and we were told about a child's "sleeping behavior," "crying behavior," or "tantrum behaviors."

In my 1971 book, *Behavior Therapy and Beyond,* I included a separate chapter on "Cognitive Restructuring," which led many behavior therapists of the day to accuse me of indulging in "mentalism," invoking "Cartesian dualism," and watering down the purity of hard-won behaviorism. Today, such views would be embraced only by extremists. Recently, in the expanded edition of their 1976 book, *Clinical Behavior Therapy,* Goldfried and Davison (1994) stated: "One no longer needs to argue for the admissibility of cognitive variables into the clinical practice of behavior therapy. Most therapists who use behavioral interventions routinely make use of cognition in their assessment and interventions" (p. 282). And they cite Craighead (1990) to the effect that more than two-thirds of the membership of the Association for Advancement of Behavior Therapy now view themselves as cognitive-behavior therapists.

The change from a "narrow-band" position to a "broad-spectrum" orientation has been evident in many circles. Albert Ellis, the founder of rational-emotive therapy, is a prime example. Initially, he called his psychotherapeutic approach "rational therapy" (RT); this was soon broadened to "rational-emotive therapy" (RET), and most recently it has been further expanded to "rational-emotive behavior therapy," (REBT). But the emphasis throughout most writings on "cognitive-behavior therapy," or "rational-emotive behavior therapy," is primarily trimodal—they refer to an A-B-C format: Affect-Behavior-Cognition. Although some sensory techniques (e.g., relaxation methods) and imagery procedures (e.g., picturing oneself quelling fearful reactions) are employed (Ellis, 1994, 1996), REBT practitioners do not devote special attention to the wide array of specific, and often very effective, imagery and sensory procedures that are available (e.g., Lazarus, 1984; Zilbergeld & Lazarus, 1987). This, in my opinion, leads to serious oversights.

To portray us as individuals who only feel, act, and think (Affect-Behavior-Cognition) overlooks the fact that we also have five senses that contribute significantly to our well-being (what I refer to as the sensory modality). And in addition to thinking, planning, verbalizing, knowing, and understanding (i.e., cognizing), we also form pictures (the imagery modality) of past, present, and future events that profoundly influence what we do, how we feel, what we sense, and how we think. So for starters, we need to expand A-B-C into B-A-S-I-C (Behavior, Affect, Sensation, Imagery, Cognition).

But the overall paradigm is still incomplete. Our behaviors, affective responses, sensations, images, and cognitions do not occur in a vacuum. We are essentially social beings. Our interpersonal relationships lie behind so many of our joys and pains and contribute so fundamentally to life's satisfactions (or the lack thereof) that they warrant a specific place in our schema. Thus, we add the interpersonal modality, yielding six separate but interactive dimensions (BASIC I.). Finally, because we are essentially biochemical-neurophysiological entities, it is crucial to include the biological modality—BASIC I.B. However, by changing the "B" to "D" for Drug therapy—because clinically speaking, our most frequent biological interventions involve the use of psychotropic medications—we have the more meaningful acronym BASIC I.D. But it must be remembered that the "D" modality stands for the entire panoply of medical and biological elements—nutrition, exercise, somatic complaints, prescribed and recreational drugs, and so forth.

PLACING THE BASIC I.D. IN PERSPECTIVE

In multimodal assessment, the BASIC I.D. serves as a template to remind us to examine each of the seven modalities and their interactive effects. It implies that we are social beings who move, feel, sense, imagine and think, and that at base we are biochemical-neurophysiological entities. The multimodal schema may be depicted as follows:

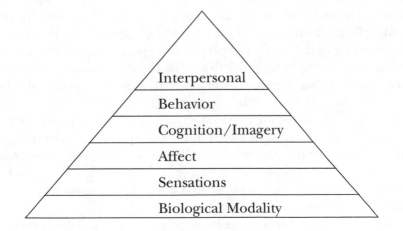

Figure 3.1 The multimodal hierarchy.

The base is "Biology" and the apex is "Interpersonal". Why? Because (as was touched on in chapter 1) a person who has no untoward medical or physical problems and enjoys warm, meaningful, and loving relationships, is apt to find life pretty good. Although the seven modalities are by no means static or linear but exist in a state of reciprocal transaction, the biological modality probably wields the most profound influence on all the other modalities. Let me state again that unpleasant sensory reactions can signal a host of medical illnesses; excessive emotional reactions (anxiety, depression and rage) may all have biological determinants; faulty thinking, and images of gloom, doom, and terror may derive entirely from chemical imbalances; and untoward personal and interpersonal behaviors may stem from many somatic reactions ranging from chemical toxins to intracranial lesions. Hence, when any doubts arise about the probable involvement of biological factors, it is imperative to have them fully investigated.

Let us say that a patient complains of aches, pains, tension, worries, frustration, and problems getting along with his father. A therapist with a systemic orientation, who hypothesizes that these complaints are probably secondary to underlying familial tensions, may immediately begin to construct a genogram—and might lose the patient in the process. Similarly, the patient may not look favorably on a therapist who regards the complaint of tension as a focal point and plunges in with a course of relaxation training. Would any therapists actually behave so preemptively? Probably not too many experienced ones, but novices often err in this direction.

Thus, any good clinician will first address and investigate the presenting issues. "Please tell me more about the aches and pains you are experiencing." "Do you feel tense in any specific areas of your body?" "You mentioned worries and feelings of frustration. Can you please elaborate on them for me?" "What are some of the specific clash points between you and your father?" Any competent therapist would flesh out the details. However, a multimodal therapist goes farther. She or he will carefully note the specific modalities across the BASIC I.D. that are being discussed, and which ones are omitted or glossed over. Areas that are overlooked or neglected often yield important data when specific elaborations are requested. And when examining a particular issue, the BASIC I.D. will be rapidly traversed. Here's an example:

THERAPIST: So you worry a good deal about losing your job.
PATIENT: I literally lose sleep over it.
THERAPIST: When you become so worried and preoccupied about your job, what would you usually be *doing* at the time?

PATIENT: Just worrying. That's what I'd be doing.

THERAPIST: I'm asking if you would worry no less or no more when out with friends, watching television, eating dinner.

PATIENT: No, I don't think about it when I'm keeping active. It happens mainly when I get into bed and try to go to sleep.

THERAPIST: And when you are dwelling on it, how do you feel? Do you become depressed, fearful, discouraged . . . ?

PATIENT: All of the above.

THERAPIST: And does your body feel tense?

PATIENT: I know I grind my teeth. My dentist calls it bruxism or something.

THERAPIST: What pictures or images come into your mind when you are dwelling on possibly losing your job?

PATIENT: I see myself as a bum, as a sort of bag man. And I can hear and see my father saying, "I always told you that you were a loser!"

THERAPIST: A loser who goes straight to the poorhouse! So do you actually tell yourself that if you got fired you'd probably end up in dire poverty, thereby fulfilling your father's prophecy?

PATIENT: No, not when I think about it rationally.

THERAPIST: That's good to know. One of the things we need to figure out is how to keep your rational thoughts from being undermined by irrational ones. But tell me, who are the people who might want to fire you, and why would they do it?

PATIENT: It's my boss's son. He's really incompetent, but his daddy owns the company and he's the blue-eyed boy. And so I am supposed to report to him and he gets mad when I go straight to his dad.

THERAPIST: So perhaps you and I need to figure out some strategies here. But tell me, what do you do if you can't get to sleep and keep on worrying?

PATIENT: I don't know what to do.

THERAPIST: I mean do you ever resort to alcohol or sleeping pills?

PATIENT: If it's really bad I take 0.5 mg Xanax that my doctor prescribed for me.

Discussion.   Traversing the BASIC I.D. usually keeps one "on target." This brief inquiry into the client's job-related worries quickly unearthed focal points for subsequent remediation.

- *Behavior:* Given the fact that he appears to dwell on his worries only while in bed, when trying to go to sleep, several behavioral interventions suggest themselves. (1) He could be induced to employ "prescribed time periods for worrying," wherein he would have preset intervals during which to fuss and brood (and he could also be advised to dwell on his worries only in one particular place). (2) He could be taught to switch on soporific images while in bed, and to leave the bedroom for 10 to 15 minutes if his negative mind-set intruded. (3) He could employ a mild aversive consequence when dwelling on the issues beyond his prescribed times (e.g., a rubber band snapped on his wrist).
- *Affect:* In concert with the other tactics employed, his negative affective reactions may be quelled by repeating various statements designed to provide self-assurance (e.g., "I will be able to cope with and survive the loss of my job!").
- *Sensation:* The use of general and differential relaxation techniques might be helpful (e.g., teaching him how to relax his entire body and then how to direct the relaxation specifically to his face and jaws).
- *Imagery:* Coping images could be prescribed wherein he pictured himself surviving the loss of his job without ending up as a "bag man."
- *Cognition:* His panic-driven thinking would be addressed, and in place of his penchant toward catastrophic ideation he could learn self-calming statements and more rational and realistic ideas.
- *Interpersonal:* His difficulties with his employer's son could be examined and possible social skills could be taught.
- *Drugs/Biology:* Instead of resorting to Xanax, he could be encouraged to apply the relaxation methods and positive imagery procedures.

It is also important to determine one's clients' strengths and to point out that they have already solved several problems in various spheres of their lives (see de Shazer, 1988). There is no need to shy away from mentioning obvious positive qualities—"You have a very pleasant way of talking"; "I like the way you combine tactfulness with honesty"; "You made clever use of distraction to prevent yourself from getting depressed."

THE TEMPORAL FACTOR

We have been discussing an anxious patient who tended to obsess about losing his job. To offset his worries, at least eight different procedures were recommended. Wouldn't this be rather time-consuming? The answer, in a word, is "no." Most of the specific recommendations would take only a few minutes to elucidate. Those that call for practice and rehearsal need not cut into the actual time spent with the client. Thus, after spending about 10 to 15 minutes in the consulting room, the necessary relaxation skills can usually be fostered by giving or loaning specially prepared or commercially available relaxation training cassettes. And cognitive restructuring is often expedited by giving, selling, or loaning specific articles, chapters, or books to clients. After perusing this material, the client and therapist spend a short but highly focused, solution-oriented, time period discussing the material and its particular relevance for the person. (Specific details and recommendations will be provided in chapters dealing with the different modalities.)

Why bother to work multimodally—why involve the entire BASIC I.D. when feasible? Follow-up studies that I have conducted intermittently since 1973 have consistently suggested that durable outcomes are in direct proportion to the number of modalities deliberately traversed. Although there is obviously a point of diminishing returns, it is a multimodal maxim that *the more someone learns in therapy, the less likely he or she is to relapse.* In this connection, circa 1970, I became acutely aware of lacunae or gaps in people's coping responses that were evident even after they had been in various therapies, often for years on end.

A striking example was that of a young psychiatrist who had undergone a 4-year training analysis in addition to other forms of psychotherapy, and who consulted me for persistent feelings of anxiety that had never abated despite his own personal and professional training. Within minutes, it was evident that he suffered from what Karen Horney (1950) called the "tyranny of the should." It is astonishing that someone can go to college, obtain a medical degree, complete a residency in psychiatry, receive years of personal therapy, and emerge utterly ignorant of one of the fundamental tenets of rational-emotive behavior therapy—that the more categorical imperatives to which one subscribes (shoulds, oughts, and musts), the more anxious, hostile, guilt-ridden, and depressed one is likely to be (Ellis, 1994, 1996). Thus, the young psychiatrist had gained many putative insights into the so-called psychodynamic aspects of his problems, but nobody had shown him how his extremely demanding attitude undermined his personal feelings and interpersonal attachments. Moreover, his lack of social skills had never been addressed, and his interpersonal style left much to be desired. He was inclined to give orders (rather than make requests), and he was quick to offer destructive rather than constructive criticism. Perhaps even worse, it was not uncommon for him to issue ultimatums. But he could wax eloquent about the interstices of the unconscious, about ego-psychology or the vicissitudes of object relations or structural theory.

Table 3.1   A Simple Modality Profile

Modality	Problem	Proposed treatment
B	"Disorganized/sloppy"	Contingency contracting
	Phobic avoidance	Systematic desensitization
	Leaves things to last minute	Time management
A	Guilt	Explore antecedents and irrational ideas
	Anxiety related to criticism and rejection	Coping imagery and rational disputation
	Sadness/despondency	Explore faulty thinking and encourage her to seek out positive events
S	Fatigue/lower back pain/ tension headaches	Relaxation training/ physiotherapy exercises
I	Loneliness images/ poor self-image/ images of failing	Coping imagery exercises
C	Dichotomous reasoning/too many/ "shoulds" overgeneralizes	Cognitive restructuring
I.	Nontrusting	Risk taking
	Overly competitive	Cooperation training
	Unassertive	Assertiveness training
	Avoids social gatherings	Social skills training
D.	Uses alprazolam p.r.n.	Monitor to avoid dependency
	Overweight	Weight-control methods (e.g., contingency contracting, self-monitoring, support group)
	Insufficient exercise	Physical fitness program

(A thorough medical examination replete with laboratory tests revealed no diagnosable contributing organic pathology.)

As his multimodal therapy (MMT) continued, it also became clear that he had only the most rudimentary knowledge of relaxation, meditation, and positive imagery techniques. Initially, he was quite incapable of applying them to himself, but he learned very quickly to quell many of his anxieties as soon as he mastered some of these methods. Had he learned these straightforward cognitive, interpersonal, sensory, and imagery procedures during his training, he could probably have averted years of needless suffering.

And so it is with many people who receive therapy that is quite excellent as far as it goes but does not go far enough. Unfortunately, there are still too many therapists who are of the opinion that their major, if not their only, task is to provide a warm, genuine, empathic relationship. Others believe that all will be well if their patients acquire dynamic insights. Meanwhile, their patients receive no precise behavioral instructions, no specific sensory exercises, few (if any) cognitive coping skills, self-empowering imagery techniques, or relationship enhancement procedures.

It is important to emphasize that it takes up very little extra time to assess and ameliorate the most salient problems across a patient's entire BASIC I.D. Follow-ups indicate that this ensures far more compelling and durable results.

MODALITY PROFILES

After conducting an initial interview and perusing a completed Multimodal Life History Inventory (Lazarus & Lazarus, 1991), it is often useful to draw up a Modality Profile that lists the main complaints in each area and the proposed treatments. For example, the profile of a 33-year-old woman who sought therapy for "anxiety and depression" revealed 22 specific (but interrelated) problems and yielded 19 remedial strategies (see Table 3.1 on opposite page).

Many multimodal therapists prefer to omit writing down the proposed treatments but focus only on the list of identified problems. Thus, another client who was hypochondriacal and suffered from somatic symptoms that medical examinations had been unable to explain—headaches, chest pains, gastrointestinal distress, and premenstrual tension—revealed 17 discrete but interactive problems.

- *Behavior.* Excessive cigarette smoking; insufficient exercise
- *Affect.* Anger/resentment/hostility (seldom directly expressed; fear (of pregnancy); fear of having a heart attack
- *Sensation.* Headaches; palpitations, stomach pains; tremors; chest pain; menstrual pain

- *Imagery.* Death images; not coping; failing
- *Cognition.* Perfectionistic; false romantic ideas; overconcerned about parental approval
- *Interpersonal.* Resorts to passive-aggressive tactics (spiteful), especially with husband
- *Drugs/Biology.* May require medical intervention for menstrual dysfunction

The Modality Profile can be modified at any time. It serves as a template to guide the therapist and as a blueprint to remind him or her not to overlook specific issues.

The multimodal (BASIC I.D.) format permits one to employ several discrete procedures that further enhance assessment and therapy. These are: (1) Bridging; (2) Tracking; (3) Second-Order BASIC I.D. assessments; and (4) Structural Profiles. These procedures will be explicated in chapters 5 and 6. First, however—in chapter 4—let us examine the relevance of theory to practice, with special emphasis on eclectic thinking versus the field of psychotherapy integration.

Theories and Techniques

$\mathbf{M}$any people have erroneously concluded that multimodal therapy (MMT) is atheoretical or, even worse, antitheoretical. Impalpable techniques applied on the grounds of random whims would hardly be a basis for advancing therapeutic knowledge. Clinicians, at the very least, have an implicit rationale for what they do. Therapeutic methods will be determined mainly by one's view of causality. If demoniacal possession is postulated, exorcism will be the treatment of choice. If unconscious conflicts are assumed to be behind most problem behaviors, conflict resolution will be the major therapeutic mainstay. Nevertheless, the relation between theory and practice is exceedingly complex. Many seem to downplay or ignore the obvious and important reality that techniques may be effective for reasons other than those that gave rise to them. Let me state this again: *Techniques may, in fact, prove effective for reasons that do not remotely relate to the theoretical ideas that spawned them.*

Scientific theories are at best an elaborate and sophisticated set of assumptions or propositions. It seems trite to emphasize that theories are not facts. Yet psychotherapists are inclined to downplay their commitment to the process of discovery in favor of the dissemination of convictions. Many luminaries in our field have strayed from the disinterested and impartial path of science into the heavily invested realm of personal politics. Philosophers and historians of science, such as Thomas Kuhn and Paul Feyerabend, have shown that even in physics and chemistry scientists are apt to be irrationally devoted to their pet theories, even when data weigh heavily against them. In the psychotherapy arena this penchant is even more pronounced. Preconceived agendas are heavily promoted, and it is unfortunate that in most instances adherence to a school is based, not upon outcome data or on established treatments of choice, but rather on personal preference.

Theories are developed to help explain or account for various phenomena. Perhaps the proper function of a theory is to try to make objective sense out of bewildering observations and assertions. In psychotherapy, a theory endeavors to answer the questions *why* and *how* certain processes arise, are maintained, can be modified, or are extinguished, and to make predictions therefrom. From a scientific standpoint, acccptable ideas are those that can be tested empirically. There are, of course, ways of arriving at facts other than through strictly objective and scientific inquiry. Intuitive, personal, relational, and aesthetic "truths" cannot be discounted. In discovering truth, any means will do. As Crews (1986) stated: "Scientific rigor properly enters the picture only when we try to ascertain whether purported laws of nature, however derived, merit our belief" (p. 107). We must studiously avoid the circular process in which a theory bespeaks a clinical approach that leads to data collection, which tends to verify the theory and invites further clinical work, which supports the theory even more.

OBSERVATIONS AND CONSTRUCTS

The difference between *theories* and *observations* is crucial. "Observations" refer to notions that call for minimal speculation. Here's an observation: "He is walking slowly; his shoulders are stooped; his eyes are downcast." To make inferences from this observation—"He seems depressed"; "He's probably trying to ward off an anxiety attack"; "I think he's very angry about something"—enters the realm of opinion and conjecture. Compare the following two statements: (1) "People overheard him arguing with his wife and then saw him kicking the garden furniture on his patio." (2) "He did so because of displaced aggression stemming from castration anxiety." The first statement (the observation) contains some low-level inferences and is not 100% theory-neutral, but the range of assumptions conveyed in the second statement makes it quantitatively and qualitatively different from the first. There are far too many therapists who are inclined to resort to "mind raping." Without due regard for objective assessment, extreme caution in the face of conjecture and speculation, and a fitting indifference toward persuasion and hearsay, only chaos and confusion will prevail.

Given the fact that observations do not occur in a vacuum but are influenced by our viewpoints (we bring our theoretical ideas to what we observe), is it in fact possible to separate observations from theories? According to extreme views of social constructionism (e.g., Gergen, 1982), we create what we observe to the extent that we cannot discover what is inherent in nature; rather, we invent our theories and categories and view the world through them. From this perspective, it is impossible to separate observation from theory. My colleague Stanley Messer and I have debated this topic rather vigorously, and he espoused a postpositivist or postmodernist conception and championed a hermeneutic perspective in place of the disciplined light of objective evaluation. The nuances of this discussion fall outside the scope of this book, and I refer the interested reader to our published dialogue (Lazarus & Messer, 1991). Held (1995) has written a most incisive critique of postmodern theory in psychotherapy. Also see Woolfolk (1992).

Although psychologists probably have no "pure" observations, the distinction between observations and theories is nevertheless worth upholding. The point at issue is that observations do not have to constitute pure facts in order to be separable from theories. If it were deemed totally impossible to separate the two, how would we ever test our theories? I might mention that from my perspective a psychodynamic heritage, when stripped of its excess theoretical baggage, allows me to appreciate the observation that people are capable of denying, disowning, projecting, displacing, splitting, and repressing their emotions, and that unconscious processes are often important for a full understanding of behavior. These remarks should not be misconstrued as giving weight to reified versions of "defense mechanisms" or the "unconscious mind."

What I have just stated flows naturally into a consideration of the question: What specific constructs are necessary to account for the vagaries of human conduct? What terms and concepts are required for an adequate psychotherapeutic framework? Do we have to postulate the existence of a soul, psychic energy, organ inferiority, archetypes, instincts, actualizing tendencies, oedipal desires, the unconscious, ego states, or an inner child? The entire profession would enjoy a completely different ambiance and much greater respectability if we fully appreciated the principle of parsimony (the view that between two equally tenable hypotheses, the simpler is to be preferred) and if we heeded Occam's razor (which holds that explanatory principles should not be needlessly multiplied).

In a broad sense, we are products of the interplay among our genetic endowment, our physical environment, and our social learning history. But this does not inform us as to exactly how, when, where, and why certain behaviors, outlooks, insights, fantasies, and interpersonal patterns are acquired. Indeed, I submit that issues pertaining to etiology and causality are poorly understood. Moreover, we do not require a precise, accurate explanation of what caused a problem in order to remedy it. In the spirit of Occam's razor, I submit that we do not have to look beyond seven constructs when accounting for the origins of psychological disturbance and their mechanisms of change.

SEVEN CONSTRUCTS

Seven factors that shape and maintain human personality are: (1) associations and relations among events; (2) modeling and imitation; (3) nonconscious processes; (4) defensive reactions; (5) private events; (6) metacommunications; and (7) thresholds.

1. Associations and Relations among Events

Rescorla's (1988) incisive update on Pavlovian conditioning called into question the necessity of paired stimuli and the relevance of temporal contiguity to produce learning. Nevertheless, throughout life, connections or associations are made between events. An association may be said to exist when responses evoked by one stimulus are predictably and reliably similar to those provoked by another stimulus. This was originally termed the "association reflex" by V. M. Bekhterev; the term "conditioned reflex" was then introduced and in turn subsequently changed to "conditioned response." Many of the phenomena of classical and operant conditioning are helpful in accounting for the presumed origins of and maintaining factors across a diverse range of human activities. Simply stated, "classical conditioning" seems to be the most parsimonious explanation of someone's aversion to orange juice upon discovering that this person's mother tried to disguise the bitter taste of certain medicines by adding orange juice to the mixtures. And "operant conditioning" seems an adequate "explanation" for a situation wherein a boy who complains of frequent headaches for which physicians can detect no organic reasons has a parent who fusses over him and cuddles him when he feels indisposed.

Without becoming embroiled in the controversies that surround them, it seems useful to draw on concepts such as "stimulus generalization," "positive reinforcement," "negative reinforcement," "punishment or aversive stimuli," "stimulus control," "intermittent reinforcement," "self-reinforcement," "successive approximation," "trial and error," and so forth.

2. Modeling and Imitation

Human survival is greatly facilitated by our ability to acquire new responses by watching someone else performing an activity and then doing it ourselves. In mastering many complex occupational tasks and social requirements, success often depends on imitation, observational learning, and identification (see Bandura, 1986).

3. Nonconscious Processes

What I am calling "nonconscious processes" are very different from the psychoanalytic notion of the "unconscious," with its putative complexes, topographical boundaries, intrapsychic functions, and elaborate but untestable inferences about personality development. The term "nonconscious processes" merely acknowledges that (1) people have different degrees and levels of self-awareness, and (2) despite a lack of awareness or conscious comprehension, unrecognized (subliminal) stimuli can nevertheless influence one's conscious thoughts, feelings, and behaviors. Both conscious experience and nonconscious psychological processes are necessary for a full understanding of the way in which human beings know, learn, or behave (Shevrin & Dickman, 1980).

4. Defensive Reactions

Who would argue against the observation that people are capable of truncating their own awareness, of beguiling themselves, of mislabeling their affective responses, and of losing touch with themselves (and others) in a variety of ways? Thus, they are apt to rationalize and overintellectualize. They may deny the obvious or falsely attribute their own feelings to others (projection). They can readily displace their aggressions onto other people, animals, or things. The term "defensive reactions" is intended to adhere to the straightforward empirical realities without embracing the added meanings given to the term "defense mechanisms" with their elaborate tie-in to complex attitudinal, perceptual, and attentional shifts that supposedly ward off overbearing id impulses.

Defensive reactions are "avoidance responses" that attenuate pain, discomfort, anxiety, depression, guilt, and shame. Thus, "sublimation" is regarded not as "the translation and modification of impulses/wishes into pursuits which are consciously acceptable to the ego and superego" (Reid,

1980, p. 84), but as a distraction, as a channeling of effort and concentration in one direction rather than another. For example, when a young man inquired how best to handle his sexual urges during the final stage of his wife's pregnancy, he was advised to masturbate, sublimate, or both. In this context, "sublimation" referred to the fact that if he exercised, jogged, and became absorbed in several activities, his sexual urges were likely to be less compelling.

5. Private Events

In the days of our neobehavioristic zeal, it was assumed that classical (respondent) conditioning, operant (instrumental) conditioning, and modeling and vicarious processes could account for most human processes. It soon became evident, however, that people are capable of overriding, by their own thinking, the best-laid plans of contiguity, reinforcements, and example. As Bandura (1986) stated, "beliefs about how probabilistic outcomes are related to actions can weaken, distort, or even nullify the effects of response consequences " (p. 129). Thus, *private events* (e.g., beliefs, values, attitudes, images, self-reflection, self-regulation) must be added to the pool of basic concepts. This includes the idiosyncratic use of language, semantics, problem-solving competencies, appraisals, attributions, self-efficacy, expectancies, goals, encoding, and selective attention. These notions point to a significant filter—people do not automatically respond to external stimuli. Their thoughts about those stimuli will determine which ones are noticed, how they are perceived, how much they are valued, and how long they are remembered.

6. Metacommunications

People not only "communicate"; they also "metacommunicate" (i.e., communicate about their communications). People can step back and examine the content and process of their own relationships and patterns of communication. They step outside the frame of the ordinary one-to-one connection. The most typical intervention involving metacommunications is in couples therapy wherein the dyadic transactions are examined by each partner. For example, when discussing Structural Profiles (see chapter 6), in addition to rating themselves, spouses may be asked, "What scores do you think your partner will give to you, and can you guess what scores he or she will give to himself or herself? " Discussions about accuracies and discrepancies in these different ratings usually enhance the process of mutual understanding.

The many books and articles on paradox and reframing all address the metacommunications that take place in all relationships and the way in which they can be used to facilitate problem solving. A nonclinical example provided by Watzlawick, Weakland, and Fisch (1974) brilliantly captures the essence of what they call "second order change." They recount an incident that took place in 19th-century Paris. An army commander and his detachment receive orders to clear a city square of rioters by firing at the rabble *(canaille)*. His soldiers take up firing positions with their rifles aimed at the crowd. There is no question that the soldiers will prevail, because they are armed and the crowd is not. Many people will be killed, and this will only further inflame the existing melee. As the commander draws his sword to signal the soldiers when to begin firing, a ghastly silence ensues. At the top of his lungs he yells: "Mesdames, m'sieurs, I have orders to fire at the *canaille*. But as I see a great number of honest, respectable citizens before me, I request that they leave so that I can safely shoot the *canaille*." The square becomes empty within a few minutes. As Watzlawick et al. point out, the commander elected to use a second-order, paradoxical intervention by *reframing* the situation in a way that was acceptable to everyone involved. As we will discuss, metacommunications can enhance the progress of therapy in many instances.

7. Thresholds

People have different frustration-tolerance thresholds, stress-tolerance thresholds, pain-tolerance thresholds, noise-tolerance thresholds, cold-tolerance thresholds, and pollution-tolerance thresholds (to name a few). Thresholds are largely innate. In other words, people respond to a wide variety of stimuli with a distinctive pattern of autonomic nervous system arousal. Those with a *stable* autonomic system (which usually goes hand in hand with high thresholds to many events) have a different "personality" from those with *labile* autonomic reactions (which usually correlates with low thresholds to many conditions or situations). The latter are anxiety-prone and are inclined to become pathologically anxious under stressful conditions (Tyrer, 1982)

I contend that the combined contributions from the aforementioned constructs account quite adequately for the range of human experiences—

our hopes, wishes, fantasies, feelings, dreams, aspirations, motivations, ambitions, fears, misgivings, loves, and hates. A question often posed at workshops, in seminars, and during various classes is whether a "spiritual" dimension should be included. In keeping with the principle of parsimony, I think it would be a mistake to view "spirituality" as a separate modality or dimension. I submit that what is referred to as "spiritual" usually consists of a combination of intense and very strong beliefs, often including vivid imagery and potent sensory components. It is advisable, at all times, to avoid the needless addition or multiplication of explanatory principles.

TECHNICAL ECLECTICISM AND EXPERIMENTALLY VALIDATED PROCEDURES

The arbitrary nature of theoretical beliefs was brought home to me circa 1964 after I had treated two patients for several months behind a one-way mirror at the Palo Alto V.A. Hospital before a professional audience from the San Francisco Bay area. At that juncture I was an ardent behavior therapist who downplayed cognitive processes. Week after week my colleagues observed me implementing relaxation procedures, systematic desensitization, assertiveness training, various imagery methods, and homework assignments. Discussions with the audience about the rationale for applying or withholding certain procedures followed each session. After 8 to 10 sessions, it was clear that the patients had made significant progress. A heated discussion then ensued as to the reasons behind the constructive changes. The audience comprised theorists from different persuasions, and each one argued vociferously for the veracity of his or her own theoretical position. Because antithetical convictions were being espoused, it occurred to me that whatever the genuine or accurate underlying processes happened to be, most of the speakers (myself included) were probably in error. Nobody disagreed that progress had ensued, but no one saw eye-to-eye as to *why* these gains had occurred.

This was the major impetus behind my development of a technically eclectic outlook (Lazarus, 1967, 1989a). As London (1964) underscored, we apply techniques, not theories, to our patients—although one's theoretical underpinnings will determine, to a very large extent, which techniques are admissible or inadmissible (see Davison & Lazarus, 1994, 1995). It makes sense to select seemingly effective techniques from any discipline without necessarily subscribing to the theories that begot them. Thus, it is not necessary to draw on a single tenet of Frankl's (1967) existential theories in order to employ his method of "paradoxical intention," and one may freely employ the "empty chair technique" without embracing any theories from gestalt therapy or psychodrama (see Lazarus, 1995). The reader who is interested in the role of theory in psychotherapy integration is referred to the incisive article by Arkowitz (1989).

In multimodal therapy, the selection and development of specific techniques are not at all capricious. My basic position can be summarized as follows: Eclecticism is warranted only when well-documented treatments of choice do not exist for a particular disorder, or when well-established methods are not achieving the desired results. Thus, if we consider the treatment of agoraphobia, with or without panic attacks, there are several well-documented, empirically established, and highly recommended treatment procedures (Barlow, 1988; Carter, Turovsky, & Barlow, 1994). For example, Barlow (1988) has stated: "Investigators around the world have demonstrated very clearly that exposure in vivo is the central ingredient in the behavioral treatment of agoraphobia and that this process is substantially more effective than any number of credible alternative psychotherapeutic procedures" (p. 407).

However, when these procedures, despite proper implementation, fail to achieve desired results, one may look to less authenticated procedures or endeavor to develop new strategies (see Davison & Lazarus, 1995). Clinical effectiveness is probably in direct proportion to the range of effective tactics, strategies, and methods that a practitioner has at his or her disposal. Nevertheless, the ragtag importation of techniques from anywhere or everywhere without a sound rationale can only result in syncretistic confusion (see Lazarus, 1989a, 1995). A systematic, prescriptive, technically eclectic orientation is the opposite of a smorgasbord conception of eclecticism in which one selects procedures according to unstated and unreplicable processes (Lazarus & Beutler, 1993; Lazarus, Beutler, & Norcross, 1992).

Recently, the vast literature on treatment regimens, in journal articles or entire books, has accentuated multidimensional, multifactorial, and multimethod approaches. Manuals written expressly for treatment application typically prescribe combinations of techniques. For example, in treating panic disorder, Barlow and his associates (e.g., Barlow, 1988; Barlow & Cerny, 1988; Barlow & Craske, 1989) recommend a combination of several components: relaxation training, respiratory retraining, cognitive restructuring, and exposure to the internal cues that trigger panic. Similarly, the treatments of choice for obsessive-compulsive disorder include exposure to the feared stimuli, and response prevention, often in conjunction with pharmacological treatment (such as serotonin reuptake blockers). The treatment of schizophrenia, in addition to antipsychotic medication, calls for social skills training, vocational rehabilitation, and supported employment, as part of the overall case management (Mueser & Glynn, 1995). Even Shapiro's (1995) Eye Movement Desensitization and Reprocessing (EMDR) is a multifaceted, if not multimodal, method that entails a careful and systematic combination of behavioral, affective, sensory, imagery, cognitive, and interpersonal inputs.

The aforementioned treatment combinations make use of no eclectic maneuvers but are all drawn from within the established purview of cognitive-behavioral interventions. There are few, if any, data or controlled studies to support the notion that clinical outcomes are enhanced by adding psychodynamic, gestalt, or any other nonbehavioral techniques or procedures to standard cognitive-behavioral methods. Nevertheless, the potential for clinical enrichment exists. It needs to be emphasized again that arbitrary blends of different techniques are to be decried. Lambert (1992) warned that certain eclectic practices "may even produce therapies that are less efficacious than the single-school approaches from which they are derived" (p. 122). Kazdin (1984) had arrived at a similar conclusion and emphasized that "premature integration of specific positions that are not well supported on their own may greatly impede progress" (p. 142). Kazdin (1996) has written an extremely cogent, comprehensive, and erudite discourse on the pros and cons of different treatment combinations. Wilson (1995) has also provided an incisive critique of psychotherapy integration. He stressed that technique selection can rest upon rather capricious, arbitrary, and subjective criteria unless proper guidelines are established.

Those who attempt to blend different theories in the hope of developing more robust techniques usually end up in blind alleys, simply because in the final analysis, basic irreconcilable differences among specific theories render them incapable of being meaningfully combined (see Appendix 5). Thus, the widespread tendency to fuse behavioral and psychodynamic theories leads only to an amalgam of superficial or phenotypical similarities due to (as Franks, 1984, brilliantly argued) fundamental incompatibilities. There are a few exceptions—for example, the merging of general systems theory with the precepts of cognitive-behavior therapy offers considerable promise (see Kwee & Lazarus, 1986), a view with which Franks (1982) concurs. Those in search of an overall theory of personality are referred to Staats (1996), who provides a unified theory of psychological behaviorism.

The cognitive-behavioral literature has documented various treatments of choice for a wide range of afflictions, including maladaptive habits, fears and phobias, stress-related difficulties, sexual dysfunctions, depression, eating disorders, obsessive-compulsive disorders, and posttraumatic stress disorders (Seligman, 1994). The *Handbook of Prescriptive Treatments for Adults,* edited by Hersen and Ammerman (1994), includes the aforementioned disorders in addition to dementia, psychoactive substance abuse, somatization disorder, multiple personality disorder and various other personality disorders, psychophysiologic disorders, pain management, and diverse forms of violence. There are relatively few empirically validated treatments outside the area of cognitive-behavior therapy (see Chambless, 1995). Two noteworthy exceptions are interpersonal psychotherapy of depression (Klerman, Weissman, Rounsaville, & Chevron, 1984) and bulimia nervosa (Fairburn, 1993). When approached by patients with problems in any of the aforementioned areas, the knowledgeable and ethical therapist will administer the established treatments of choice (or refer the patient to someone well versed in the necessary procedures who is likely to expedite and ensure the most rapid and durable treatment results).

We now return to the specific methods that constitute the essence of brief but comprehensive therapy—the multimodal way.

CHAPTER 5

Multimodal Assessment Procedures:

Bridging and Tracking

All the methods that have been developed in the multimodal approach have one major objective in mind—to expedite and enhance the treatment trajectory. I opened my book *Multimodal Behavior Therapy* (1976) with the following four words: "Most therapists waste time." Twenty years later, having seen many more novice and expert therapists in action, I would reiterate these same sentiments. Whether listening to tapes of my supervisees or watching demonstrations by accomplished authorities in the field, I often find myself impatiently drumming my fingers and wishing they would get to the point or do something truly helpful. Perhaps what I may consider to be "the point," or consider especially "helpful," another clinician may perceive as irrelevant, so let's discuss actual events rather than talk in generalities.

I was observing the videotape of a well-known therapist who was proudly demonstrating his methods. The hour-long tape comprised the highlights from a condensation of five consecutive sessions. His client, a 24-year-old man whose primary problem revolved around his poor work record, had been fired for insubordination four times in 6 months. His significant computer skills kept him highly employable even in a tight job market, but his belligerent attitude to authority figures was having unfortunate results. The video depicted a detailed exploration of the client's reactions to his overbearing father, the supposed nucleus of his maladaptive responses to authority figures. Toward the last third of the tape (presumably after some 4 hours of actual dialogue had elapsed) the same ground was still being traversed over and over again. (It was like watching a carpenter persistently hammering a nail again and again to no effect instead of putting it in the right place and using power tools.) On several occasions the client said, "I think I understand why I react the way I do, but I may need to learn a different style, a better way of expressing myself." From my perspective, behavior rehearsal or role-playing seemed strongly indicated. In today's market we can ill afford the luxury of going over the same material for 5 hours—some managed health concerns may permit the patient to be seen for a total of only five or six sessions!

While listening to the audiotapes of my students' therapeutic endeavors, I often become impatient. Recently, one of my trainees was interested in examining her client's feelings about an insulting remark. If she knew what her client was feeling, she would be able to assess the client's emotions and help her deal with them. Instead of discussing her feelings, the client kept referring to her thoughts and opinions and introduced extraneous matters. The trainee kept badgering her, although gently, to stop analyzing the situation but to reveal and explore her feelings. They were going round and round and were simply wasting time. Here's a (slightly edited) transcript of their interaction:

TRAINEE: When your mother called you a liar in front of your uncle, did this hurt your feelings? How did it make you feel?

CLIENT: I think my mother was grandstanding. This was intended to impress her big brother.

TRAINEE: At your expense? How did you feel about that?

CLIENT: I know my uncle regarded my mother as too lenient and had said something about that in the past. She admires him, really looks up to him. So I think she was trying to prove to him how tough she was.

TRAINEE: So she turned round and called you a liar. Didn't that bother you?

CLIENT: You have to understand the relationship between my mother and my uncle. His opinion counts a lot to her.

TRAINEE: I understand that, but you're not answering my question.

CLIENT: She has another brother, and with him she is completely different.

TRAINEE: Let's not get off the subject. I'm trying to understand your feelings and emotions. So are you telling me that your mother's remark didn't bother you at all?

CLIENT: The point is that I was not lying. I really was telling the truth.

TRAINEE: I believe that—that's the whole point. So there you were being falsely accused of lying, and this was said in front of someone else. Didn't you feel upset or something?

CLIENT: My mother's really a very insecure person. Perhaps you should get to meet her some time.

TRAINEE: That's getting off the subject again. Look, you were called a liar when you were not lying. Moreover, your mother said this to you in front of another person. This is not an isolated instance. Your mother often calls you names and makes false accusations. So I'm asking if you find yourself feeling very hurt by this, if you feel really angry, or anxious, or depressed, or confused, or whatever.

CLIENT: Well, I've tried to explain the dynamics of the situation to you.

At this juncture I switched off the tape, told my trainee that her client was suggesting a potentially profitable avenue (meet the mother and perhaps see mother and daughter together for a few sessions), and inquired why she thought the young woman seemed so reluctant to discuss her feelings. Their rapport appeared to be good, and the event under discussion did not seem to be so highly significant or affectively laden as to be especially threatening (two obvious factors that can account for a client's reluctance or refusal to open up feelings). My trainee said that her client had an extremely inquiring mind and was apt to dwell on reason rather than emotion. I then proceeded to teach the trainee a simple method called "bridging" that often proves helpful when clients are reluctant to discuss or reveal important feelings.

BRIDGING

When clients are disinclined to talk about feelings but offer rationalizations and intellectualizations, one of the least productive methods is to lock horns and pester them to express their emotions. The bridging technique consists of entering the client's preferred mode (cognitions) and after a few minutes, asking about a different (presumably more neutral) modality (e.g., imagery, or sensations). Thus, after perhaps the fifth or sixth attempt, instead of persistently trying to extract affective material, the trainee could have joined the client in her cognitive mode. Instead of saying, "That's getting off the subject," the dialogue may have proceeded more or less as follows:

TRAINEE: So she is so interested in looking—what is it?—strong, or together, that she says things that disregard your feelings to impress her one brother.

CLIENT: Yes. She wants him to see her as someone who is not a pushover, who knows how to handle her kids and does not let them get the better of her.

TRAINEE: So it seems like a good idea to keep one's distance when she is in the company of people like that brother of hers. That's neither the time or the place to discuss any touchy issues with her.

CLIENT: You've got that right!

TRAINEE: In addition to your uncle, are there also other people to whom you mother kowtows?

[The dialogue could continue at this level for several minutes. In this way, the client is likely to feel validated and heard, and would not have a sense of being pressured. The therapist can then switch to a modality that is perhaps less threatening, such as sensory reactions.]

TRAINEE: By the way, while we have been discussing these various points, have you noticed any sensations anywhere in your body—such as any tension, or warmth, or flushing, thirst, trembling—anything at all?

CLIENT: My neck feels tight.

TRAINEE: Do you notice any other sensations?

CLIENT: My jaw muscles also feel tight and my right shoulder hurts a bit.

TRAINEE: Let's just get into those sensations for a while—tight neck and jaws and shoulder pain. Can you describe them to me?

[They have now exited from the cognitive modality, and the focus is on sensory reactions. In other words, they have *bridged* out of cognition into sensation. After discussing various sensory responses for as little as 30 to 60 seconds, one can attempt to bridge into affect.]

CLIENT: . . . and the tense feelings in my neck also seem to radiate down my shoulders and I can even feel a tightness in my back.

TRAINEE: I guess the entire matter we have been talking about is tension-producing. Does the tension translate into any feelings or emotions? What do you *feel*? What are you experiencing emotionally?

CLIENT: I have two feelings. I feel mad, and I feel sad.

TRAINEE: When your mother called you a liar, would you say that you felt mad or angry and sad or depressed?

CLIENT: Yes. I feel let down by my mother.

TRAINEE: That's important. Let's look into that.

Comment: In many cases, 5-minute detours along the lines suggested by the foregoing hypothetical exchange enable one to sidestep various barriers and rapidly arrive at a productive point instead of wasting time haranguing the client or arguing. The sequence is straightforward:

1. If the client seems unwilling to enter into a particular domain (most often the affective modality), join him or her in what appears to be a preferred area of discourse.
2. After a few minutes, attempt to move into a different modality (e.g., sensation or imagery by asking "Do you notice any sensations?" or "Are you aware of any images or pictures in your mind's eye?")
3. In most cases, a shift into a different modality is readily forthcoming.* Remain in this zone for a short time (no more than a couple of minutes) and then try to bridge into the affective modality.

Here is a verbatim transcript of a bridging maneuver in which Imagery was used as a backup before briefly moving into sensations and then eliciting affective reactions:

CLIENT: I don't know. I mean do you think she had the right to, um, sort of just, you know, dump me like a sack of potatoes.?

THERAPIST: Yeah, I know what you mean. It hurts.

CLIENT: It's not as though . . . you know, not like I deserved it or anything.

THERAPIST: Not at all. You were aboveboard.

CLIENT: I really was. It's like, I don't know how to put it, um, sort of like being stabbed in the back.

---

*If the client does not shift modalities, remain in the first area and try shifting or bridging a few minutes later. If this still proves unsuccessful, abort the mission and suggest a different tactic. "Let's come back to this subject at another time. How would you like to practice some different relaxation exercises now?" Thereafter, if time permits, one might try bridging once again.

THERAPIST: So it's pretty painful. What's the main feeling you have emerged with? Is it anger, or is it sadness, or something else?

CLIENT: Well, in a way it did not come as a complete surprise. I mean to say that she had done this before and she was sort of unstable, if you know what I mean.

[Given the client's apparent reluctance to discuss his feelings, bridging commenced at this point.]

THERAPIST: [Joining the client in the cognitive modality] When had she done this before?

CLIENT: When? All I know is that she had mentioned walking out on others. I had asked her why she couldn't work it out with them or discuss it rather than just splitting, but I never got an answer. Yeah, I sort of expected it in a way.

THERAPIST: But it was still a sort of shock. What's her case? I mean, why does she do this sort of thing, in your opinion?

CLIENT: I dunno. I guess she gets bored after a while or something. [Pause] It's not like we had a falling out or anything. Do you remember that time, I think I told you about it, when we went over to Kenny's house for dinner?

THERAPIST: Was that when you had that tiff in the car?

CLIENT: That's it. Well, let me tell you what happened afterwards. I don't think I gave you the follow-up.

[The dialogue continued for approximately 3 minutes, during which the client elaborated on the theme that he had been, in many respects, long-suffering and that the relationship was doomed from the start. When the client stated, "I can just see it all happening before my very eyes," the decision to bridge into the imagery modality seemed appropriate.]

THERAPIST: So can you picture the scene and describe it to me? Why don't you close your eyes, take your time, and tell me what you see?

CLIENT: [Closes his eyes] I see her body language and the dress she is wearing. I can see the expression on her face, like a sort of a smirk. She is sort of staring at me. [Pause of about 20 seconds]

THERAPIST: Can you use a zoom lens to study her eyes and the message in them?

CLIENT: [Opens his eyes] That's funny. As you said that, I sort of saw right through her. What's that word? Misogynist?

THERAPIST: That's a woman-hater.

CLIENT: Okay, so she is whatever's the word for "man-hater."

THERAPIST: You're rubbing your neck. Is it hurting?

CLIENT: Yeah, it's tight.

THERAPIST: Are you aware of any other sensations apart from the tightness in your neck?

CLIENT: Yeah. My head hurts right here [pointing to his right temple] and my chest feels tight. I guess talking about this stuff makes me uptight.

THERAPIST: Well, it's upsetting.

CLIENT: I guess so.

[This appeared to be a good moment to see if access to his affective modality could now be gained.]

THERAPIST: So what's the main feeling you've come away with?

CLIENT: I feel like a prick, like a damn fool. I'm such a trusting . . . so sort of so gullible, that I walk into situations with my eyes open but they may as well be shut. I knew from the start what, or who, I was dealing with. That pisses me off, you know!

THERAPIST: Whom are you so angry with?

CLIENT: Myself!

THERAPIST: Well, let's see if we can avoid your tendency to dump all over yourself. It seems that this can be chalked up as a useful learning experience.

Having discussed bridging, let us now turn to a different assessment method that also expedites therapy and keeps it on target—*tracking*.

TRACKING

Most people appear to have a "firing order" that is fairly stable across situations and over time. Thus, when an agoraphobic woman in her early forties was enabled to realize that she tended to generate anxiety in a predictable sequence, the appropriate treatment progression became evident. Careful questioning by the therapist revealed that she first dwelled on unpleasant *images* (e.g., picturing herself fainting in the street—although this had never happened—and seeing herself involuntarily urinating in public, although this had never happened to her either). These negative pictures were evoked whenever she contemplated being alone in a public place, especially when shopping at a supermarket or venturing into a mall. The disturbing images, in turn, immediately aroused unpleasant *sensations* (e.g., tachycardia, trembling, difficulty breathing, and a ringing in her ears), whereupon she would start thinking that she was potentially psychotic (*cognition*). This I-S-C sequence or "firing order" (Imagery-Sensations-Cognitions) usually culminated in a sense of pervasive anxiety and sometimes resulted in a full-blown panic attack.

A former therapist had employed relaxation techniques (i.e., a Sensory method) and in vivo desensitization (a behavioral process), but with limited benefits. The fact that her trigger points were in the imagery modality indicated that some "right-brain" input would be most effective as a first line of intervention. Other methods would probably have a less significant impact. The client confirmed this impression. Upon receiving the relaxation and exposure therapy, she said: "I became more relaxed when strolling down the street outside my house. We live in a very quiet neighborhood. But the moment I thought of going anywhere more public, I became terrified. Now I understand why this was so. Those pictures of fainting and urinating which were sort of in the background would take over. I never realized this is what was happening until you asked me to look for actual pictures in my mind."

Given her I-S-C- firing order, the treatment sequence in this case first applied a range of coping images. In sessions and at home, she would practice a progressive series of excursions in which she visualized herself staying calm in larger and more crowded public situations. She was also schooled in an anti-fainting procedure—"If you feel faint or light-headed, immediately tense your body and keep the pressure up." As an interesting aside, she soon overcame her fear of fainting, but her anxiety about urinating in public proved extremely stubborn, whereupon the suggestion was made that when venturing out, she might consider wearing special padded apparel designed for incontinent people. Granting this client permission to use this "therapeutic crutch" facilitated risk-taking and further expedited the desensitization process. She complied and at this juncture in vivo exposure plus relaxation training proved highly effective.

The *tracking* procedure is typically employed when clients are puzzled by inexplicable affective reactions. The usual themes are: "These feelings seem to come out of the blue." "I don't know why I feel this way." "I don't know where it's coming from." Clients are asked to recount the latest incident.

Thus, a client who reported having repeated panic attacks "for no apparent reason" was able, after simple questioning, to put together the following string of events.

Her most recent panic attack occurred while watching television. She became aware that her heart seemed to be beating louder than usual (sensory awareness). This brought to mind an episode where she had recently passed out at a party. (She had imbibed too much alcohol and felt dizzy and light-headed at the time.) The memory (image) of this event still occasioned a strong sense of shame. Thus, the heightened heartbeat together with her picture of disgrace, coupled with concern from friends at the party, accentuated her untoward sensations. She soon feared that she was going to pass out again, and this induced her sense of panic—an S-I-C-A pattern (Sensation, Imagery, Cognition, Affect). Thereupon, treatment pinpointed the two triggers—sensation and imagery. She was first taught a series of calming techniques ranging from muscle relaxation to reassuring self-talk. Next, she was desensitized to the affective sequelae surrounding the image when she overdrank at the party. This bimodal intervention appeared to extinguish her symptoms of panic.

On occasion, the tracking procedure simply calls for the identification of a triggering modality that sets in motion a range of other associations and responses. Here is a case in point. What follows is a tracking sequence with a client who was perplexed about certain feelings of sexual embarrassment:

CLIENT: I mean it's crazy, really crazy. I mean I know up here [pointing to his head] that in a sexual situation a woman probably feels flattered when a man has an erection. But if I see her looking at my erection, I feel, how do I say it, sort of bashful, kind of foolish and embarrassed. Like I say, it's crazy. So I can make love in the dark. It's fine if she *feels*, but she mustn't *look*. Is that crazy or what?

THERAPIST: It's not crazy, and you're not crazy. There's usually a straightforward explanation for these feelings.

CLIENT: Well, it sure as hell doesn't make sense to me. You know, when I was about 20 I went out with this woman and we were necking in the car. I was aroused, and she noticed the bulge in my pants. She kind of giggled and said something like, "Oooh! Look what I see!" I felt awful, sort of like I'd been caught red-handed at some crime. I lost my erection instantly. I told this to a shrink when I was in college, and he said maybe my mother walked in on me when I was a kid and found me masturbating and I caught hell from her. But I can't remember anything like this. I mean if it had happened, wouldn't I be able to remember it?

THERAPIST: Probably. Let's try a method I call "tracking." Let's start with the opposite of what you anticipate. Imagine yourself with an erection and three women see it and exclaim that you are wonderful and how impressed they are.

CLIENT: [Erupts into laughter]. No, I can't do that.

THERAPIST: Why not? What would happen?

CLIENT: [Still laughing] It's so funny.

THERAPIST: What's so funny about it?

CLIENT: [Breathless from laughter] It's hard to put it into words.

THERAPIST: What would happen? Would they run out of the room? Would they get angry? Would they attack you sexually?

CLIENT: [Grinning] They'd probably think I'm a sexual maniac. Just kidding.

THERAPIST: Well, how about that? Any guy with a hard-on is a sexual maniac?

CLIENT: [The chuckling stops, and he becomes thoughtful] Jesus! I just had a flashback. [Long pause]

THERAPIST: A flashback?

CLIENT: Yeah. It's funny how this just came back to me. [Pause]

THERAPIST: Don't keep me in suspense.

CLIENT: Jesus. It must go back to when I was about 14. One of my friends was in the hospital for an appendectomy. He was about 16 at the time. Well, he told me this story about the nurse shaving him before surgery, you know, shaving his pubic hairs. So she was holding his penis and putting shaving cream on his groin and he got a hard-on. So she had a rubber mallet handy and each time he got hard she hit the shaft of his dick with this little hammer which made the erection go down. [He begins to laugh] I don't know if he was just kidding, you know, putting me on, but I mean I remember thinking how incredibly embarrassing this must have been. I cringe when I think of it even now. I mean, what must that nurse have thought? And the whole idea of having a rubber mallet handy. . . I don't know. [Pause]

THERAPIST: So if he had not become erect, what would this have meant? I mean, would you see this as a good thing?

CLIENT: Well, then he would not have made a fool of himself. Look at it this way. Here's a nurse just doing her job. She's not interested in having sex with the guy and his pesky erection is just in the way and has to be gotten rid of. He gets treated like a bad child. I mean he gets whacked—popped right on the dick!

THERAPIST: So are you implying that through some weird association this story left an indelible impression on you which transformed every woman into a nurse and you into a patient?

CLIENT: It obviously goes deeper than that, but it's a good beginning. But I never made any connection until now.

THERAPIST: So if you conjure up the image of the nurse, the pubic hairs, the shaving cream, the rubber hammer [pause] what happens? What do you feel or sense or see?

CLIENT: I need to think about that.

Comment: In this instance, the goal was greater self-understanding rather than specific behavior change. By focusing on different images, a "flashback" (so-called forgotten memory) was elicited. It should be noted that the entire procedure took about 3 minutes. The use of bridging and tracking saves time by keeping the therapy targeted, focused, and relevant to the issues under discussion. These procedures often pinpoint salient trigger events in the problem matrix. As a homework assignment, the use of tracking permits clients to unearth relevant problem sequences between sessions. They learn how to intervene on their own and are enabled to evaluate their attempts at self-help.

In chapter 6 we turn to additional methods of assessment that also achieve these ends.

Multimodal Assessment Procedures:

Second-Order Basic I.D. and Structural Profiles

T herapy can easily get bogged down. Sometimes progress can come to a halt for reasons that elude the understanding of even highly perceptive and knowledgeable therapists. When this occurs, a recursive application of a BASIC I.D. assessment may often break the impasse.

SECOND-ORDER BASIC I.D. ASSESSMENTS

An extremely unassertive 32-year-old man was receiving social skills training with a view to speaking his mind and developing a capacity for appropriate confrontation when called for. The usual role-playing, coaching, exhortations, and modeling were all to no avail. He remained as passive as ever and allowed himself to continue being subservient to his wife, exploited by his siblings, and intimidated by his employer. When asked why he thought it was so difficult for him to develop assertive responses, the client said, "I have no idea. I guess I'm just a hopeless case."

A Second-Order BASIC I.D. was applied. When converging on a recalcitrant problem and examining it across the seven modalities, important information often comes to light. Thus, the client was asked to imagine that a magic pill had rendered him truly assertive, and he was invited to expound on how he would *behave* under those circumstances. He said that he would upbraid various people for what he regarded as their unfair or inconsiderate treatment of him. "And how would you *feel?*" He stated that his predominant feeling would be one of resentment and anger. In the *sensory* modality he would experience "a surge of energy" pulsing through his body. His *imagery* showed a number of contrite but respectful relatives and friends, and his *cognitions* included such sentiments as "I am strong, secure, and self-sufficient."

The first five modalities revealed little of importance, but when the *interpersonal* area was more closely examined, a hitherto unexpected and unrecognized pattern emerged. As we entered this domain, the client was unable or unwilling to continue with the exercise. "You have just ingested yet another magic pill," he was told, "and you have no choice but to be assertive with every person you encounter." The client grew silent and pensive. He broke the silence by declaring, "It just wouldn't work!" He explained that he had merely played along with the exercise, given lip service to it, while traversing the first five modalities, but that an escalating sense of discomfort had nevertheless grown within him. What transpired was a view that assertive expressions would have two dire consequences. First, they would escalate into aggression and probably lead to violence. Second, acting assertively would inevitably destroy the goodwill he received from his significant others. He stated that his success, such as it was, rested on the love that others had for his accommodating ways, and what they saw as his good-natured compliance (his proclivity to *assent* rather than to *assert*).

Before embarking on the usual assertiveness training techniques, the important differences between *assertion* and *aggression* had been carefully spelled out. Nevertheless, the Second-Order Assessment revealed that two factors required greater attention: (1) his aggressive-violent proclivities, and (2) his need to appreciate that an assertive stance, if stylistically appropriate, was by no means likely to undermine any love, caring, or devotion that he was apt to receive from others.

Once again, in the interests of brief, targeted, focused therapy, a procedure that took no more than a few minutes had placed the therapy back on track.

Here is an example of a Second-Order BASIC I.D. Profile. The client had an established alcohol addiction, and one of the items on his Modality Profile was "Urges to Use Alcohol or Cravings." When he was asked about the impact of these urges or cravings across the BASIC I.D., the following emerged:

- *Behavior:*   Clenches jaw
                     Starts pacing or wringing hands
- *Affect:*   Anxiety
                     Anger
- *Sensation:*   Muscle tension
                     Dry mouth
                     Vague uneasiness in pit of stomach
- *Imagery:*   Visualizes drinking alcohol
                     Imagines smell and taste of drink
                     Pictures sense of intoxication
- *Cognition:*   Thoughts of unfairness
                     Belief that craving will never subside
                     Idea that intake can be controlled
                     Various other rationalizations
- *Interpersonal:*   Withdraws from social interaction or
                     lashes out irritably at others
- *Drugs/Biology:*   Smokes a cigarette or has a cup of coffee

Thus, addressing key problems makes meaningful change more likely to ensue. When studying this Profile, several points for intervention become evident. The most obvious strategies might include (1) more attention to deep muscle relaxation, (2) success images of turning away from alcohol, and (3) cognitive disputation. The typical scenario in a nonmultimodal treatment arena would be for a clinician to offer some interpretative comments when a client expresses powerful cravings, or to provide some off-the-cuff coping techniques. The Second-Order BASIC I.D. pinpoints the important idiosyncratic variables and leaves little to chance. It adds both precision and brevity to clinical interventions.

STRUCTURAL PROFILES

People tend to favor some BASIC I.D. modalities over others. Thus, we may speak of an "imagery reactor," a "cognitive reactor," or a "sensory reactor." This does not mean that a person will always react in or favor a given modality, but that there is a tendency to give emphasis to certain response patterns. If someone's most highly valued representational system is visual, she or he is inclined to organize and respond to events in terms of mental images. On the other hand, someone who is deeply analytical (cognitive) may be unable to form more than fleeting visual images. This type of information may assist one in (a) selecting appropriate techniques, and (b) identifying the modalities that are most relevant for generating improved functioning.

Structural Profiles differ from Modality Profiles (as outlined in chapter 3). Modality Profiles list problems across the BASIC I.D., whereas Structural Profiles yield a quantitative assessment that can readily be compiled by means of a simple rating scale.

The following directions are given. "Here are seven rating scales pertaining to various tendencies that people have. Using a scale of 0 to 6 (6 is high—it characterizes you, or you rely on it greatly; 0 means that it does not describe you, or you rarely rely on it), please rate yourself in each of the seven areas."

1. *Behavior.* How active are you? How much of a doer are you? Do you like to keep busy?

   Rating: 6 5 4 3 2 1 0

2. *Affect.* How emotional are you? How deeply do you feel things? Are you inclined to impassioned or soul-stirring inner reactions?

   Rating: 6 5 4 3 2 1 0

3. *Sensation.* How much do you focus on the pleasures and pains derived from your senses? How tuned in are you to your bodily sensations—to food, sex, music, art?

   Rating: 6 5 4 3 2 1 0

4. *Imagery.* Do you have a vivid imagination? Do you engage in fantasy and daydreaming? Do you think in pictures?

   Rating: 6 5 4 3 2 1 0

5. *Cognition.* How much of a thinker are you? Do you like to analyze things, make plans, reason things through?

   Rating: 6 5 4 3 2 1 0

6. *Interpersonal.* How much of a social being are you? How important are other people to you? Do you gravitate to people? Do you desire intimacy with others?

   Rating: 6 5 4 3 2 1 0

7. *Drugs/Biology.* Are you healthy and health-conscious? Do you take good care of your body and physical health? Do you avoid overeating, ingestion of unnecessary drugs, excessive amounts of alcohol, and exposure to other substances that may be harmful?

   Rating: 6 5 4 3 2 1 0

Despite the arbitrary and subjective nature of these ratings, useful clinical information is often derived. When inquiring about the meaning and relevance of each rating, important insights are often gained regarding an individual's style, manner of thinking, and emotional needs. Scores on a Structural Profile also tend to provide clues for technique selection—for example, clients with high ratings in "Imagery" but low scores in "Cognition" are likely to respond better to visualization methods than to the usual methods of cognitive restructuring. The different modality "firing orders" that people display (see chapter 4) are usually in accord with their ratings on a Structural Profile. In couples therapy, it can prove illuminating for partners to compare their respective ratings and also to anticipate what scores their spouses would attribute to them. Thus, we have yet another rapid method of gaining understanding and facilitating therapeutic progress. Rudolph (1985) clearly demonstrated how the use of Structural Profiles facilitates the clinician's awareness of when to dwell mainly on the individual client, the couple, or the family. For example, significant dyadic discrepancies usually require couples to be seen together to iron out the meaning and relevance of their respective ratings.

A 35-item Structural Profile Inventory (SPI) has been developed. (See Appendix 2.) The SPI evolved by generating a variety of questions that, on the basis of face validity, appeared to reflect essential components of the BASIC I.D. Factor analytic studies gave rise to several versions of the questionnaire until one with good factorial stability was obtained. Additional research demonstrated the reliability and validity of this instrument (Herman, 1993; Landes, 1988, 1991). It tends to save time when couples fill out the SPI. The scores frequently generate meaningful discussions and promote a better mutual understanding while pinpointing specific differences and areas of misunderstanding .

The use of the Expanded Structural Profile developed by C. N. Lazarus (see Appendix 3) has proved to be extremely useful. Clients who are reluctant to complete the extensive Multimodal Life History Inventory (Appendix 1) are usually willing to fill in the Expanded Structural Profile. Couples appear to find the exercise illuminating, as it clarifies similarities and differences that can lead to clash-points. Moreover, it can be used to enhance compatibility.

Applying the measures, methods, and procedures outlined in this chapter and in chapter 4, is likely to keep therapy on target, relevant, and focused, and thus to expedite the aims of short-term but comprehensive and effective psychotherapy.

CHAPTER 7

Some Elements
of Effective Brevity

$\mathbf{I}$f therapy is to be brief but effective, one cannot afford prolonged impasses. The clinician needs a repertoire of tools for getting therapy back on track whenever detours or digressions arise. In this regard, Omer (1994) has presented many excellent strategies for overcoming impasses and for dealing with cases that get stuck. It is imperative to know how to restart the engine when therapy becomes stalled. In many respects, the methods discussed in chapters 5 and 6—Bridging, Tracking, and Second-Order BASIC I.D. Assessments—fall into this category. By incorporating these procedures when necessary, therapy is apt to remain solution-centered. Most important, however, is the need to set clearly defined goals very rapidly and to move into specific problem-solving tactics as soon as possible. Budman (1994) advises therapists to take their best shot in the first session, because it may be the only one that the client pursues. The interested reader is referred to the writings of Nicholas Cummings, who is undoubtedly at the forefront of managed health care and brief therapy (e.g., Cummings, 1985, 1988, 1991; Cummings & Sayana, 1995).

FAXES, E-MAIL, TELEPHONES, AND LETTERS

If therapy is to be brief but effective, it seems to me that therapists need to think about their clients in between sessions. It is necessary to review one's "game plan," to determine if there is evidence of progress, if there have been any oversights, or if "course corrections" are indicated (to throw in a different metaphor). Thus, when a colleague announced that she sees 50 individual patients a week, I rather indelicately remarked, "That tells me that your clients are getting shortchanged." I have always kept my case-load down to manageable proportions, leaving time for reflection, self-examination, and contemplation. When reading the notes or musing over some interactions in a session that has taken place a day or two ago, I often get in touch with the client if I discern a point that needs to be made, if I discover potential grounds for misunderstanding, if I change my mind about a particular homework assignment or wish to add another, or if the client is in the midst of a critical situation that warrants a sym-pathetic inquiry. Depending on the circumstances, I have made extensive use of phones, faxes, letters, and e-mail for this purpose. Of course, if the matter is affectively loaded or somewhat delicate, I always make sure that the client will retrieve a fax transmittal himself or herself, and because I believe that the Internet is easily invaded, I couch my letters through this medium in such a way as to remain discreet. Unlike a lawyer, I do not levy a fee for these services but regard them as part and parcel of the original fee for service. This tendency to "go the extra mile" usually pays huge div-idends in expediting therapeutic progress. It models conscientiousness, inspires hope, and emphasizes an action-oriented philosophy for prob-lem relief.

There is generally a downside to most endeavors. A minority of clients may take unfair advantage of this clinical largesse by trying to become pen-pals or by corresponding at length on the Internet instead of coming in for sessions. This is grist for the mill and can readily be managed. In my experience the pros most definitely outweigh the cons and provide a stan-dard of care that expedites the entire treatment process.

WASTE NO TIME

Some caveats that were handed to me as a student made no sense back then and make even less sense today. For example, we were warned: "Diag-nosis must precede treatment, so don't intervene prematurely." "A com-plete history must come before the application of any therapeutic technique." On the contrary! This only wastes time. For example, within 2 minutes of an initial interview I might say, "You seem very tense. Am I correct about this?" The client's affirmation may then lead me to say, "Before we talk about your issues, may I show you a quick but effective breathing and relaxation method? " If the client appears responsive and interested, I will take a few minutes to show him or her how to use diaphragmatic breathing, coupled with deep muscle relaxation. This is apt to calm down the client so that he or she then becomes more responsive to the rest of the session, and it sets the stage for brief therapy by (a) equipping the client with a useful strategy, (b) forming a didactic and solution-focused mind-set, and (c) informing the client that the therapist is equipped with specific tools that can readily be learned.

When a client declared during an intake interview, "I don't know if I have the right to be happy," before exploring the basis of this negative appraisal, I wasted no time in pointing out that if I failed to convince him 100% of his inalienable right to happiness simply on the basis of being human, the end result was likely to be less than satisfying. Among the drawbacks to brief therapy have been the Freudian zeitgeist and Hollywood movies that lead clients to expect detailed psycho-excavations into their past while they do little more than free-associate. During the days of almost unlimited economic resources, I would refer those clients who desired prolonged introspection to a psychoanalytic practitioner. Nowadays, under managed health care, such luxuries can rarely be indulged in. The mentality of "let's first talk for a year or two and get to know each other before getting down to business" pretty much belongs to a bygone era. (This point is discussed in greater detail in chapter 11.) Educating the client to be able to benefit from brief therapy therefore is often a first priority. A point that cannot be emphasized enough is that *the outcome of therapy can be influenced significantly by what the client is led to expect.*

THE EDUCATIONAL THRUST

Bibliotherapy, to be pedantic, can be extremely useful. If a picture is worth a thousand words, certain books are not worth a thousand sessions—but they can expedite therapy enormously. I have given copies of the book *I Can If I Want To,* which I wrote with Allen Fay in the 1970s and which is still in print (Lazarus & Fay, 1992). It emphasizes that

> *Human beings, unlike any other species on earth, have the unique capacity for instant change. People are capable of making immediate and long-lasting decisions that can have a profound influence on their emotional well-being. In other words, even if someone has responded incorrectly or "neurotically'" to a given situation for many years on end, a systematic corrective exercise can often undo the problem there and then. (p. 16)*

This little book also addresses myths about change, underscores that therapy is education, shows how much unhappiness is self-created, and discusses why many people don't change. (Also see Lazarus, Lazarus, & Fay, 1993.)

Adopting a didactic stance in which clients practice homework assignments often requires priming from the therapist. The following sorts of statements prepare clients to participate in the healing process: "If you wished to achieve physical fitness, you would not attain it merely by reading books on the subject, talking about it, and thinking about becoming physically fit—you would have to *do* certain things such as exercise and adhere to a sensible diet. If you wanted to learn to type or to play a musical instrument, here again, a lesson a week without active practice during the week would achieve very little. And so it is with psychotherapy, which is really a form of applied psychology, and form of emotional muscle-building. The things you do, and the actions you take and make between sessions, will decide if you derive benefits or simply mark time."

From my perspective, clients need to be disabused of the widespread overvaluation of insight. The notion that for therapy to be effective, it must explore the past and develop links to the present remains deeply rooted in our culture and is still being perpetuated by short-term psychodynamic psychotherapists. The data suggest otherwise—that methods that rely mainly on guidance, skills training and problem solving are empirically more effective than conversational therapy (Chambless, 1995).

Many therapists cling to the mistaken belief that they need to know a tremendous amount about a client before they can intervene meaningfully and effectively. They strongly resist the fact that one does not have to know almost everything about the client to be truly helpful. This can prove particularly frustrating when the client is a mental health professional. I recently treated a woman who is a practicing psychologist. Her managed health concern had allowed nine sessions. After the initial meeting I felt that we would only need three or four. My assessment strongly indicated that she needed to acquire some assertive responses in dealing with her husband and children, who tended to take unfair advantage of her. She, however, given her psychological training, insisted on telling me, in needless detail, the background factors in her family of origin that contributed to her nonassertive proclivities. My tactful attempts to move on and to focus on the here and now were being obstructed by her. At the start of the fifth session I commenced with a focused lecture. First, I challenged the notion that change requires one to know the reasons behind one's behavior. Then, I disputed the view that it takes a long time to change and strongly attacked the myth that rapid changes are superficial and won't last. Finally I emphasized that psychological and behavior change calls for problem solving and the acquisition of new responses in the here and now rather than preoccupation with the heretofore. "If you accept these premises," I added, "we can move on and attain our goals. If you disagree with what I have said, nine sessions will prove to be wholly inadequate." She seemed to get the message, and we focused on her current familial passivity. (She was adequately assertive outside her nuclear family.) When she came for her ninth and final session, she said "Bingo! Touchdown!" and told me how gratifyingly she had changed and how, in addition to herself, her husband and children were benefiting.

Therapy is not likely to be brief or effective unless strategies such as setting clearly defined goals, rapidly identifying key problems, and formulating an effective treatment plan are implemented. If therapy is viewed as education, the need for a good lesson plan becomes no less important in the clinic or the consulting room than in formal didactic or pedagogical settings.

Many therapists argue that because the doctor-patient relationship is so pivotal, it is necessary to build rapport before the client will develop sufficient trust to accept a therapist's observations, let alone to carry out assignments. In my experience, alliances can be developed very rapidly. Often, making full use of halos and placebo effects will allow instant rapport to be easily attained. Thus, when I refer someone to a colleague, I tend to give him or her a big buildup. I do not lie or distort, but I accentuate the most positive features of the referral. "Dr. Frank is both a school psychologist and a clinical psychologist, so he will be in an excellent position to advise you about your son's ADHD problem. He is also an excellent couples therapist, so he can be most helpful in dealing with the issues in the marriage. And he has seen a lot of people over the years and has often succeeded in helping those who were not helped by previous doctors." "I am referring you to Dr. Prince, who recently obtained her doctorate from Rutgers University. She was one of my best students and is very bright and extremely well trained. Please realize that we accept only about 8 students each year into our clinical training program from over 400 applicants. You can appreciate that these hand-picked 8 are the cream of the crop. So when I tell you that Dr. Prince, in my view, was number one in her class, this is really saying something." In essence, if the referral is handled in this way, lengthy rapport building is often superfluous.

Nevertheless, despite an impressive buildup, skillful promotion of the halo effect, and one's most ardent efforts to establish a positive working alliance, hate at first sight may triumph. I have referred people to colleagues whom I regard as first rate and highly credentialed, only to be told, "I took one look at Dr. E and realized that I wouldn't give him the time of day, let alone tell him my intimate life history." I feel sure we have all had experiences of this nature. It used to be argued that these so-called "negative transferences" are worth resolving, and that to do so would be in everyone's best interest. I have always entertained doubts about this view, on the ground that some people are simply too incompatible to develop a productive liaison and work successfully with one another. This perception was strongly reinforced by Herman's (1991, 1992) finding that client-therapist similarity on the Multimodal Structural Profile Inventory is highly predictive of the outcome of psychotherapy. In brief or short-term therapy, if client and therapist do not "hit it off" in the first two sessions, a judicious referral is strongly indicated.

Hitting it off, establishing rapport, developing trust, forming a close working alliance—this is necessary but often insufficient for achieving significant therapeutic gains. Within the context of a good doctor-patient relationship, it is usually necessary to take reparative action. Chapter 8 will discuss simple but powerful modes that can turn people's lives around without wasting time. Passive and reflective therapists are anathema to the process of brief and effective psychotherapy.

ELEGANT SOLUTIONS

In numerous publications, Albert Ellis has stressed the difference between *feeling better* (which is often palliative) and *getting better and staying better.* At the very least, the latter entails the abandonment of categorical imperatives—shoulds, oughts, and musts. It also requires the development of *unconditional self-acceptance* (USA) and the mitigation of *low frustration tolerance* (LFT). Ellis's development of what he now refers to as rational-emotive behavior therapy is the culmination of more than half a century of research and practice and represents one of the major contributions to the field of psychotherapy. His book on brief therapy (Ellis, 1996) is a tour de force and brilliantly sets out his major philosophy of life and therapy. Ellis has had a substantial impact on my own thinking and experience. Consequently, anyone who has been through a course of multimodal therapy will be exposed to many of Ellis's ideas—especially when working in the cognitive modality.

For example, when one of my clients was stating how desperately she needed a vacation, and how many other accoutrements she construed as essential to her happiness, I pointed out that she was confusing her needs with her desires and delivered the following speech:

> *Well, let's talk about some of your needs. Perhaps everyone's greatest need is for oxygen. If someone shuts off your air supply, you'd soon grow desperate, and if it were not rapidly restored, you'd be dead. That's a real need! And you sure need water or liquid. Without it, you'd also die. And ditto to food and sustenance. But you don't need love and respect from your children—you wish for it, desire it and want it, but you can live with or without it. And you don't need your husband to help you around the house. You would prefer it, you would like it, you want it, and you'd probably appreciate it. But I repeat, it is not a basic need. And you don't need a vacation. You very much want one. As long as you define your wants as needs, you will feel desperate if they are not met or fulfilled. If you are deprived of a luxury vacation and you equate this with being deprived of oxygen, food, or water, you'll feel downcast, sad, angry, anxious, and depressed. But if you can say, "I don't need it, I can take it or leave it, I can live with or without it, but if possible I'd like to have it," you will avoid a sense of desperation and manage to approach the matter calmly and rationally, and thereby most probably end up getting what you want . (Lazarus, 1995a, p. 85)*

The foregoing intervention led to a significant turning point in the client's life. In most instances, I have found this type of didactic coaching superior to the Socratic approach that Ellis and his followers seem to prefer. The end result of a successful course of REBT and MMT would find clients sharing a great deal in common. Nevertheless, I submit that the client who had received MMT would have a broader range of coping responses at his or her disposal, simply because a greater range of sensory and imagery techniques would probably have been taught, and more attention would have been devoted to subtle and obvious nuances of interpersonal relationships. In the sensory modality, for example, in addition to the usual methods of relaxation training, biofeedback procedures, and sensate focus exercises, MMT clinicians are apt to give homework assignments that tap into augmenting one's pleasures from other tactile, olfactory, auditory, gustatory, and visual stimuli. Be that as it may, the MMT format presents a versatile and flexible modus operandi for effecting widespread changes and provides both novices and experienced clinicians with an ongoing "blueprint" for selecting techniques and styles that best suit the needs of individual clients. Observe Ellis and his followers in action, and you will see basic similarities across sessions, situations, and individual clients; observe a multimodal therapist in action, and you will perceive a diversity of styles that are geared to the idiosyncratic needs of different and differing clients and to particular clinical exigencies.

TOWARD AN EGOLESS STATE OF BEING

Albert Ellis inspired me to develop a strategy for mitigating global self-ratings in clients with overgeneralized self-appraisals who suffer from self-blaming and self-damning propensities (Lazarus, 1977). The problem is that many clients place their "ego" on the line, thereby developing overgeneralizations that result in the bulk of anxiety, depression, and guilt-related reactions from which so many suffer. Instead of viewing oneself as possessing a unitary "self" that amounts to one's *total being,* it is important to tune into a plurality of "selves" across numerous situations. Thus, "I am useless!" is a self-statement that implies zero value in all areas of life—useless as a sibling, a son or daughter, a spouse, a parent, a friend, an acquaintance, a colleague, a moviegoer, a tennis player, an oyster-eater, a TV-viewer, and a music-lover, plus innumerable other roles that constitute the "self."

In place of the widespread proclivity to place one's entire being on the line, a simple technique can often counterbalance this unfortunate tendency. Thus, a client who had extreme anticipatory anxiety over a speech he was to deliver was addressed as follows:

THERAPIST: Instead of saying "I am giving a speech," think of your "self" not as one big *"I"* but as a whole complex of little iiiiiiiiiii-iii's. Each little "i" corresponds to some facet of your being. So instead of saying "I am giving a speech," consider the fact that *you* are not on trial. It's not the total you. Think instead: "i am giving a speech."

CLIENT: So if it goes poorly, instead of saying, *"I* gave a bad speech," it would be "i gave a bad speech." It's not *me* but merely a small part of me.

THERAPIST: Correct! But if you want to go one better, try leaving the big "I" and the little "i" out completely. You can say: "A bad speech was given." Or: "The speech was not very good." Make it task-oriented. Keep your "self" out of it completely. The goal is to have as many positively reinforcing little i's as possible.

Once this client saw that he was staking *everything* on how well he gave a public talk—his self-acceptance, the esteem of his friends and acquaintances, his job, his entire future—we were able to make progress.

Little "tricks of the trade" can go a long way to speeding up the course of therapy.

CHAPTER 8

Activity and Serendipity

T he theme of this chapter is that brief therapy usually calls for an active, directive therapeutic stance. One of the biggest myths pervading a good deal of the literature on psychological treatment is that therapists should not give advice. Karasu (1992), in a wide-ranging book that dispenses a good deal of wisdom, albeit from a psychodynamic perspective, is emphatic about this point:

> *The therapist, unlike the internist or surgeon, deliberately does not intervene to solve the patient's problems or even advise the patient to proceed in a particular direction. He or she avoids recommending what actions to take, however tempting this may be, such as persuading a patient to dissolve a troubled marriage, encouraging him or her to quit a job, or directing him or her to be more assertive or sexual. (p. 211)*

In direct contrast to Karasu's position, London (1964) a true visionary, pointed out that "action therapy" often calls for arguments, exhortations, and suggestions from therapists who are willing to assume responsibility for treatment outcomes. He stated:

> *Either therapists can successfully influence behavior or they cannot, and they have little choice of what to claim. If they wish to say that they cannot do so, or may not do so in just those areas where human concern is greatest, and are therefore not at all responsible for the behavior of their clients, one must ask what right they have to be in business. (pp. 14–15)*

Karasu, like many theorists, overlooks the fact that a good deal of emotional suffering does not stem solely from conflicts but is the result of *deficits* and missing information (see chapter 1). When hiatuses and lacunae result in maladaptive psychological patterns, no amount of insight will remedy the situation—it demands a system of training whereby the therapist serves as a coach, model, and teacher.

The major issue is to decide when certain methods are likely to be helpful or harmful. With whom, and under what circumstances, is it advisable to be active and directive, and with whom is it inadvisable to offer advice or to assume a directive stance? *Never* to intervene actively because "the moment the therapist takes a stand, he or she will disturb the intrapsychic balance of the patient's conflict " (Karasu, 1992, p. 212) is precisely the type of reasoning that decimated the enrollment in analytic training institutes and led to the advent of brief psychodynamic therapy. As Messer and Warren (1995) state in their scholarly exposition on the subject,

> *Most forms of brief psychodynamic therapy require a more active stance by the therapist than does long-term psychoanalytic therapy, in order to channel the therapy in the area of the dynamic focus. [This may include] direct confrontation of patient's defenses, which requires a rather bald show of therapist authority and assertiveness. (p. 46)*

It distresses me when therapists embrace an "always-never" philosophy instead of determining when and when not to behave in a certain way with particular individuals. Thus, as I outlined in my paper on "being an authentic chameleon" (Lazarus, 1993), I was consulted by a 42-year-old stockbroker for help with work options, conflicts with his wife, and feelings of personal insecurity. Any active interventions—e.g., attempting cognitive restructuring, suggesting a role-playing sequence, or venturing to provide homework assignments—met with a puzzled facial expression and less than enthusiastic cooperation. Even empathic reflection seemed to occasion a sense of impatience in the client. It dawned on me that he wanted a good listener—period. Accordingly, I heard his tales of woe, nodded my head intermittently, and forced myself to refrain from offering any observations, reflections, advice, or suggestions. I was intrigued when he would stress how helpful an earlier session had been, one in which I had said virtually nothing. "You really helped me put things in perspective. I've decided that the best thing to do when my wife criticizes me is not to fight back, but to apologize if I think she's right, and simply to ask her for data when I think she's wrong." He also reached his own solutions in other problem areas. Shall we conclude that *all* clients should be treated in this manner, and that one should eschew active interventions across the board? Hardly! Why is it that although one of the first things taught in Psychology 101 is that we are all unique, when it comes to the practice of certain psychotherapists one would imagine that we all come from identical molds?

Good therapists will take certain calculated risks. Here are two cases in point.

CASE 1: THE FELINE FIX

Allow me to state once more that therapists who eschew giving advice and who avoid making suggestions are likely to miss many opportunities to be truly helpful. And some extremely simple solutions can have far-reaching benefits.

A 49-year-old woman stated that she and her husband had recently moved to New Jersey and that the absence of friends and the resultant loneliness were "very depressing." She worked for 4 to 5 hours a day at a kindergarten, but her husband was extremely busy and his work demands kept them apart for the majority of their waking hours. She had married late, and they were childless despite many medical (fertility) interventions over the past decade. "I'm too old to think about having kids now," she said, "and neither of us wants to adopt."

I can envision many a therapist who would offer this woman no more than empathy, and after providing good listening skills would feel that his or her therapeutic obligation had been fulfilled. I took a different tack. "Why don't you get a pet?" I inquired. "We've thought of getting a dog," she replied, "but it just seems like too much trouble. Frankly, I don't relish the idea of walking a hound at all odd times of the day and night." "So why not get a cat?" I asked.

The very next day she went to a local animal shelter. "As I walked into the place," she said, "I swear that this tabby cat smiled at me. I know cats don't smile, but Mimi and I definitely made eye contact. I patted her and she licked my hand and purred. It was instant bonding. I took her home and that night she snuggled on the bed between my husband and me, and this has become a nightly ritual. My husband also adores this little person in a cat's body. I can't wait to get home from work to play with her and to cuddle with her. Mimi loves to sit on my lap or to nestle by my side. When I cook dinner she keeps me company—she loves to sit on the kitchen table and seems to watch over me." I studiously avoided challenging any of her anthropomorphic assumptions.

A serendipitous breakthrough occurred when she took the cat for a veterinary checkup. In the vet's office she met two women who were also cat lovers. They struck up a conversation and my client, remembering some comments I had made about risk-taking, suggested that they might want to meet for coffee. She took down their phone numbers and within a month found them both to be good friends. Fortunately, when they ventured out for dinner with their respective spouses, everyone had a good time and new friendships were established.

At this juncture, we had met for three sessions. "I don't think I need to see you any more," she said. Indeed, she was no longer lonely or depressed. I asked for a follow-up report within a month. She called with a glowing account. Mimi had become an integral family member and was a constant source of joy. Her husband had introduced them to another "delightful couple" whom he had met through his work. "We now have three couples who are fun friends and so we always have someone to visit or to go out with over weekends. So I would say that we already feel very much at home." About a year later I saw her in a supermarket, and we had a brief chat. "You performed a miracle on me," she concluded.

After this meeting I faced certain misgivings that I had harbored all along. What would happen if Mimi died? Were our three therapy sessions merely palliative? Had she learned anything of enduring value? Throwing caution to the winds, I called her and put the foregoing questions to her. One sentence stood out for me. "I can tell you something," she said, "and that is: Mimi or no Mimi, I will never be without an animal again, and I have a surefire way of making new friends."

CASE 2: PHYSICAL FEATURES

A completely different situation arose when I was consulted, circa 1970, by a woman in her early twenties who had seen several therapists to no avail. Her presenting problem was what she termed "pervasive depression." She volunteered that she had been taking 150 mg of Tofranil for the past month but that she had noted no benefits. When asked if she could recall a time when she was nondepressed, she said perhaps prior to age 4 or 5. She was lonely, felt inadequate, was socially phobic and withdrawn, and reported a history of rejection from her peers. I asked, "Is there anything you enjoy?" She replied, "I 'm a marathon runner, and just about the only time I feel at peace is when I run, which I do almost every day." She volunteered that she was probably trying to run away from the world and from herself.

As I listened to her tale of woe, I was struck by the fact that this young woman had protruding and discolored teeth, an enormous and bulbous nose, and virtually no chin, or a receding one at best. I tactfully inquired whether she had been teased by anyone, and she made my task easier by stating that she had always been considered ugly. Many people can do little or nothing about their degree of attractiveness versus unattractiveness (even with massive reconstructive maxillofacial surgery), but a large proboscis, misshapen teeth, and a receding chin are all eminently correctable. Dare one address such issues in an initial interview?

I continued discussing her history of depression, her family background, her lack of self-acceptance, and her solitary lifestyle. Her feelings toward her socially adept younger brother were also considered. I kept on wondering how she would feel if I drew attention to her nose, teeth, and chin. Would I appear superficial, sexist, or insulting? (Incidentally, this is not gender-specific—I have drawn the attention of many male clients to correctable defects in their attire or physical appearance.)

I asked about her previous therapists. What had they focused on? Sibling rivalry; her somewhat narcissistic mother; her absentee father; her dreams and fantasies. It appeared that none of her therapists had made any reference to her physical appearance. I decided to take the plunge. I did so by delivering a short talk on social inequities, pointing out that women, far more than men, were victims of a misplaced societal emphasis on good looks and physical appearance. Defensively I said, "We all know that beauty is skin-deep, but nevertheless, good-looking women have a decided advantage in life." Had she launched into a diatribe over this unenlightened and superficial emphasis, or had she countered with the notion that "beauty is in the eye of the beholder," I might have demurred. When she said, somewhat pensively, "Yes, I agree. The pretty girls get all the prizes even if their heads are filled with cotton," I took the plunge.

"If I may say so, you have three features that could turn your life around if they were rectified. Plastic surgery to your nose and chin plus some cosmetic dentistry could make a world of difference." I felt very tense while making these remarks and was greatly relieved and encouraged when all she said was, "Who could afford it?" I ventured the opinion that perhaps a letter to her insurance company from a psychiatrist and me, pointing out that this was not mere cosmetic surgery performed for reasons of vanity, but was psychiatrically essential, might impel her medical insurer to foot the bill. Once more, however, serendipity played a role. I discussed this case in one of my classes and a student mentioned that her uncle was a gifted plastic surgeon in the area who would probably be willing to provide the services at a drastically reduced rate. A few weeks later I was informed that all arrangements had been completed. I then went overseas for about a month. Shortly after my return, I called the client, who said that she had undergone plastic surgery and was in the throes of having her teeth capped. "I'll be in touch," she said.

About a month later I was told that a young woman was in the waiting room and wanted a few moments of my time. A neatly dressed and attractive young woman smiled at me as I walked into the waiting area. I introduced myself and said something like, "You wanted to see me?" She seemed amused and asked if I had forgotten who she was. I inquired if we had met before and then realized who she was. I must have uttered an expletive! It was amazing. How interesting that a few altered centimeters can render such a striking change to the human physiognomy. I expressed my astonishment. We chatted for a while. "I may need some therapy in the near future to learn how to handle the dating game," she said. "It's all so new to me."

I took another risk by asking her how she felt about the fact that she was the same person except for the fact that now she had a pretty face. I remember her exact words. "Let's put it this way—I'm not depressed or lonely anymore, and one has to accept life the way it is." This was, from my point of view, to quote the title of Talmon's (1993) book, a single-session solution.

The foregoing case leads me to emphasize that many problems articulated in therapy are compounded by the reluctance of well-intentioned therapists to broach what clients have already accepted as fact. Thus, progress is retarded by assuming that trenchant and direct disclosures will further injure an already fragile customer. My position is that refractory avoidance patterns, self-consciousness, mistrust of others, and diminished self-acceptance often take root in relationship patterns that display dishonesty and superficiality, thereby hampering self-acceptance. To break these patterns, therapists need to collaborate with clients where and how it counts.

The point of this chapter is to underscore the view that existential excursions, Rogerian reflections, Freudian interpretations, and the like will do very little to promote rapid change in people who undergo such treatments. Many years ago, Karl Menninger (1958), in the preface to his book *Theory of Psychoanalytic Technique*, stated: "Surely the continued development of our knowledge will help us find quicker and less expensive ways of relieving symptoms and rerouting misdirected travelers" (p. xi). It can be said, without fear of contradiction, that we have reached that point in time.

CHAPTER 9

Two Specific Applications:

Sexual Desire Disorders and Dysthymia

T his is probably a good point to demonstrate how brief multi-modal therapy can be adapted and applied to specific disorders. I have selected two problem areas that many therapists encounter—sexual desire disorders and dysthymia.

As Rosen and Leiblum (1995) pointed out, the types of problems addressed by sex therapists have changed considerably since the publication of Masters and Johnson's (1970) *Human Sexual Inadequacy*, when anorgasmia in women and rapid ejaculation in men were the most common and prevalent sexual disorders in therapy clinics here and abroad. Perhaps because of the abundance of sex manuals and the availability of public information, today we see far fewer sexually naive or inexperienced clients, but in recent years sexual desire disorders have increased in frequency and significance. In fact, Rosen and Leiblum (1995) state that "hypoactive sexual desire (HSD) is a major focus of . . . the field of sex therapy generally" (p. 4). This is certainly reflected in my own private practice, and I have therefore elected to discuss what Lief (1977) termed "inhibited sexual desire" (IHD) to illustrate my approach to brief but comprehensive therapy.

Similarly, what was once called "neurotic depression," but is now subsumed under the DSM-IV category of Dysthymic Disorder is also frequently encountered by therapists of all persuasions, and I will explicate how I think this condition can be handled briefly but thoroughly.

INHIBITED SEXUAL DESIRE

Clinicians frequently encounter clients who report a loss of sexual interest after a history of moderate to considerable desire and activity. What has been termed "inhibited sexual desire" may be a product of numerous etiological conditions. For instance, medical disorders, especially urological or gynecological conditions, may result in diminished sexual interest. Other factors—such as hormonal deficiency; medications (e.g., certain antihypertensive agents); the overuse of alcohol, sedatives, or narcotics; and the side effects of some psychotropic drugs—can all be implicated. Depression also tends to undermine the sexual appetite, and the range of psychological factors interfering with sexual desire is extensive. Among the most common are anger and hostility, guilt, conflict, religious prohibitions, fears about intimacy, and issues pertaining to responsibility, rejection, pleasure, and commitment. Severe stress and situational anxiety are also associated with truncated desire.

Issues in Disorders of Sexual Desire

Typically, a multimodal assessment of any problem rapidly amasses a wealth of data exceeding the thoroughness and diagnostic scrutiny of most other orientations. When the BASIC I.D. is applied to disorders of sexual desire, the following issues are explored:

- *Behavior.* Can specific response deficits or excesses be identified? Are there issues related to sexual skills and performance (e.g., kissing, caressing, massaging, and other forms of stimulation)? What are the details concerning masturbation, oral-genital contact, and the impact of situational variables?
- *Affect.* Is there evidence of anxiety, guilt, depression, anger? Are there aversions to any body parts or functions? Is there love, affection, or caring? Are there signs of displaced affect being deflected from a parent onto a partner or spouse? Are there any specific fears of intimacy?
- *Sensation.* Is there pain (e.g., dyspareunia, or postcoital discomfort) or an absence of pleasure (e.g., anorgasmia, or ejaculation without sensation)? Is self-stimulation unpleasant, neutral, pleasant, or nonexistent? Is there arousal but limited or no pleasure?

- *Imagery.* Do thoughts of sexual encounters conjure up positive, negative, or intrusive images? Are there spontaneous seductive or erotic mental images? Can specific fantasies increase or decrease sexual desire? What are the frequency and content of erotic dreams (if any)? Do books, pictures, or erotic films stimulate any arousal or desire?
- *Cognition.* What connection is there between the client's ethics, morals, and religious beliefs and his or her own sexuality? What is the client's basic sexual outlook? Are there clear-cut attitudes and sex-role expectations? Which "shoulds," "oughts," and "musts" are self-imposed, and which are placed on the partner? Is there misinformation or lack of sexual information?
- *Interpersonal relationships.* How assertive and communicative is the client? Is there a specific relational problem (e.g., a lack of attraction to the partner), and/or is there evidence of generalized interpersonal difficulties? Does power enter into the equation? Who have served as sexual role models? What are the details regarding initiation and refusal of sexual activity? Is there any history of sexual trauma—rape, coercive incest, parental censure?
- *Drugs (biological factors).* Does the client ingest any prescription medications? Does he or she use drugs or alcohol? Are there any urological or gynecological dysfunctions? Do endocrinological tests seem warranted? Have other organic factors been ruled out?

The foregoing questions provide the basis for more detailed explorations into specific areas that may call for elaboration and clarification.

When examining human sexuality, it seems clinically advantageous to think in terms of desire, arousal, stimulation, orgasm, resolution, and satisfaction because each of these phases may present discrete problems:

1. *Desire.* Here, the most common entity is "inhibited sexual desire," which is characterized by low or no interest in any form of sexual activity.
2. *Arousal.* Arousal deficits refer to the absolute or relative absence of penile tumescence (erection) or of the vaginal lubrication and distention necessary for coitus.
3. *Stimulation.* Typical problems that may arise during the stimulation phase include no erection, loss of erection, rapid ejaculation, insufficient vaginal lubrication, and loss of interest or desire prior to orgasm.
4. *Orgasm.* Orgasmic difficulties include anorgasmia, pain, diminished sensation, and ejaculation without sensation.

5. *Resolution.* Resolution difficulties include such factors as extreme postorgasmic lassitude or fatigue, depression, headache, or genital pain or discomfort.

6. *Satisfaction.* Difficulties with satisfaction refer to a negative subjective evaluation of the sexual experience, or deficits in the overall level of gratification or fulfillment that follows from the sexual experience.

Case Presentation: Inhibited Sexual Desire

The following case presentation will demonstrate and illustrate the processes and methods of brief but comprehensive therapy employed in the assessment and treatment of diminished sexual desire.

Lisa and Al.   Lisa, age 35, and Al, age 37, had been married 8 years at the time of intake. Lisa stated (and Al agreed) that during their premarital period (approximately 8 months), sex had been frequent and passionate. As soon as they were married, Lisa noticed an attenuation in Al's interest, but the frequency and quality of their sexual interactions nevertheless remained satisfactory for about 2 years. At that juncture, Al evidenced erectile difficulties, and he consulted a psychiatrist, who attributed the problem to undue work pressures. (Al's responsibility on the job had intensified, and he felt harassed much of the time.) Soon thereafter he accepted a new position that removed many of the previous work demands, and his potency was restored—but never to its former level. Over the next 4 years, intermittent problems (erectile difficulties, rapid ejaculation, nonspecific prostatitis) progressively undermined Al's sexual interest and desire. For the past year, he reported having no spontaneous sexual desire, and Lisa stated that during this time they had had sex "less than 3 or 4 times at most."

Al held a master's degree in electrical engineering and had a managerial-cum-technical position with a large company. Lisa had a master's degree in library science but worked as an advertising representative and freelance copywriter. They had no children, although for the past 2 years Lisa had felt that a final decision had to be reached, since her "biological clock" was running out. Al seemed highly ambivalent in this regard.

Al's Background.   Al had a sister 3 years his junior with whom he had fought "like a cat and dog" and from whom he felt "disconnected." He described his father as "passive" and called his mother a "battle-ax." He said, "She was often on the warpath, and at an early age I learned how to keep out of her way." When asked whether he had felt loved as a child and whether he had been shown affection and warmth, he stated that despite his father's passivity and his mother's aggressiveness, he had received adequate love and attention from both parents. He regarded them as sexually inhibited—the subject was never discussed in the home. He had learned the facts of life from peers when he was 11, at which time he started masturbating. At age 16 he started dating, and although he engaged in heavy petting on dates, his first intercourse was at age 20 with a prostitute. Over the next 8 years he had several "serious relationships," but it was only when he met Lisa, when he was almost 29, that he considered marriage for the first time. "I had never seemed to see eye-to-eye so closely with anyone. . . . We laughed at the same things and agreed about everything from agnosticism to our taste in art."

Lisa's Background.   Lisa had a sister 9 years her senior, to whom she had always felt very close. Lisa excelled academically and was favored by her father. Her parents tolerated each other, and the home atmosphere was one of "serenity but no real joy." Her mother often voiced the view that a wife has to "second-guess" her husband and see to it that she remains in control. When Lisa was about 14, her mother received a small inheritance, which "through some cunning and some luck, she managed to turn into a large sum of money." Her mother's financial independence seemed to drive a wedge between her parents. When she was 19, Lisa's mother confided in her that the father was having a clandestine love affair—a fact that her mother seemed to find amusing rather than threatening or annoying. "During my junior year at college, my parents got divorced, and during my senior year they each remarried."

Lisa was popular in college and dated frequently, "but I hung onto my virginity until the end of my senior year." Soon after graduating, at age 21, she married a man 10 years her senior. "He was super-brilliant, and I was attracted to his intellect." Nevertheless, they had few common interests; Lisa never found him physically attractive; and within 2 years they had grown so far apart that they "simply drifted into a divorce." Thereafter, while she dated several men, it was not until meeting Al that she "fell in love." She described him as "brilliant like my first husband, but infinitely more attractive and sexy."

The Multimodal Assessment.   The foregoing information is a summary of the more salient points that emerged from *two* intake interviews with the couple. At the end of the initial interview, Lisa and Al were each asked to fill out a Multimodal Life History Inventory (Lazarus & Lazarus, 1991) and to return it at the second meeting. (Some people are disinclined to fill out the questionnaire in detail because they feel that it may reveal incriminating information. We therefore tell many of our clients to omit their names, addresses, and other identifying information.)

It seemed that Al's background had rendered him especially sensitive to aggression (real or imagined) from women. He reacted to Lisa, who thought of herself as "assertive," as a person who was extremely "controlling and aggressive." In describing Lisa on the Multimodal Life History Inventory, Al had written: "She treats me like a moron. One would assume that I lacked the intelligence to compose a business letter or remember simple everyday things." Lisa, in turn, had written: "Al is just too laid back at times, and I think he views any affectionate nudging as a critical attack." During the fourth conjoint session, Lisa stated, "Look here, you two, I want answers and I want them now. I think I've been patient far too long!" I asked Lisa whether this was an example of her "affectionate nudging." I also inquired whether or not it represented her usual style when frustrated. At the end of the session, the following points of agreement had been reached: (1) In general, Lisa was inclined to "come on strong." (2) Al tended to overreact and was needlessly hypersensitive to real or imagined slights from most people, especially from women, and most of all from Lisa. (3) When feeling under attack, Al, instead of asserting himself, almost always withdrew (thereby adhering to tactics that had functional validity when he was a child but no longer served him as an adult).

Al alleged that Lisa had been openly derisive and hypercritical of his sexual inadequacies. "When I first had that problem with impotence about 6 years ago, you should have heard the things she said to me!" Lisa retorted, "That was over 6 years ago! Have I said anything since then?" Al replied, "You don't have to. It's more than evident by your actions." Lisa turned to me and said, "That's his main problem; he's so damn negative. Al's forever reading aspersions and contempt into just about everything I say or do." Al responded by saying, "Lisa, I may be too sensitive, but I'm by no means alone in regarding you as very pushy and too damn controlling. Your own sister remarked that even as a kid you liked to take charge, to be in command, to dish out orders. And didn't Sue and Phyllis and your whole tennis group call you the "great dictator"? And how many times has Gordon [her boss] been on the verge of firing you for insubordination? It's not all in my head. Sure, I may be too touchy, but you're one hell of a tough cookie." I interjected, "Just like your mother?" to which Al responded, "Yeah, but at least I could get away from her." I said, "Al, I think you and I should meet alone a few times, man to man, so that we can more closely examine your withdrawal tendencies, your wish to get away from tough situations instead of facing them and beating them. And Lisa, I would like to meet with you individually for a while to see if you might benefit by acquiring a different interpersonal style. Al, Lisa, how does this one-on-one idea grab you?" They both replied, "Fine."

Before embarking on individual sessions with me, the couple was asked to employ sensate focus twice a week. I strongly impressed upon them that these encounters were to be relaxed, affectionate, unhurried, sensual massages that excluded the involvement of breasts and genitals, and explicitly did not include any coitus or orgasms. I ascertained that Lisa particularly enjoyed receiving foot massages, whereas Al enjoyed back rubs, and I obtained a firm agreement that they would give each other pleasure in this manner twice weekly. Separate individual sessions with Al and Lisa were scheduled for the following week.

Individual Sessions with Al. Prior to seeing Al individually, I had drawn up the following Modality Profile.

- *Behavior:*   Withdrawal tendencies
- *Affect:*   Anxiety (over attaining an erection)
                   Anger (mostly unexpressed)
- *Sensation:*   Tension (mainly in jaws, shoulders, and neck)
                   Discomfort in scrotum (during bouts of prostatitis)
- *Imagery:*   Pictures (vivid memories) of negative sexual experiences
- *Cognition:*   Perfectionistic tendencies
                   "I can't stand criticism."
                   Concerns and expectations about performance
                   Conflicted about becoming a father
- *Interpersonal:* Communication dysfunction (does not state sexual preferences explicitly)
                   Unassertive (especially in expressing anger)
                   Overreacts to aggression, especially from women
- *Drugs/Biology:* Recurrent bouts of nonspecific prostatitis

Al read through the Profile and agreed that it pinpointed his main areas of difficulty. After discussing a logical starting point, we agreed on the following: (1) Al would read, most thoroughly, the first chapter of Zilbergeld's *Male Sexuality* (1978), which deals with significant myths about sexuality and helps men modify unrealistic expectations. (Lisa and Al were treated before the publication of Zilbergeld's *The New Male Sexuality, 1992*).

(2) We would address his withdrawal tendencies and his basic lack of assertiveness. (3) He would be taught specific relaxation procedures and given cassettes for home use.

Assertiveness training commenced with the usual behavior rehearsal and role-playing procedures, but soon uncovered a host of subjective dangers that characterized Al's perceptions about adopting an assertive stance in life. To Al's way of thinking, it was safer to withdraw, to remain silent, and (if necessary) to retaliate in a passive-aggressive manner when criticized or when placed in any compromising position. The basis of this pattern appeared to be a consequence of contending with his aggressive mother while at the same time identifying with his passive father.

Accordingly, time-tripping imagery was employed as follows: While reclining on a comfortable chair, Al was given standard relaxation instructions and then asked to close his eyes and imagine a scene in which he, as an adult, stepped into a "time machine" and went back in time to significant encounters with his mother. The following dialogue (taken from a slightly edited transcript of the session) ensued:

THERAPIST: You can stop the time machine and enter your life at any time in the past. Can you imagine that clearly?

CLIENT: Yes. [Pause] I remember a time, oh, I was about 5 or 6, and I had done something to enrage my mother, I forgot what, but I was playing with some toys in the den and she came in, kicked the toys all over the room, and yelled at me.

THERAPIST: OK, now you enter the picture at age 37. You step out of the time machine and into the den. See and hear your mother yelling. [Pause] Look at 5- or 6-year-old Al. [Pause]. What's happening?

CLIENT: My mother and little Al don't seem to be aware of me; they don't notice me.

THERAPIST: Well, can you make your presence felt? How would you like to gain their attention?

CLIENT: By strangling my mother! [Chuckles]

THERAPIST: Can you picture yourself handling the situation *assertively*? You are 37. Little Al is 5 or 6. How old is your mother?

CLIENT: She's about 28 or 29.

THERAPIST: Fine. Now there's no point in telling her who you are, that you are 37-year-old Al on a visit back from the future. Instead, how about simply telling her that she is mistreating 5-year-old Al?

CLIENT: [A 30- or 40-second pause] Yes, I can put her in her place.

THERAPIST: Good. In a few moments, let's discuss what transpired. But before you leave that scene, can you say something to little Al?

CLIENT: [Pause] I really don't know what to say to him.

THERAPIST: Why not reassure him? Tell him that he's a good kid, and explain to him that his mother's a bit unstable, but that he shouldn't take it to heart when she flies off the handle.

CLIENT: [Pause] Okay. In retrospect, I can tell little Al, "The battle-ax means no harm."

THERAPIST: Excellent. Now are you ready to step into the time machine and return back here?

(Additional examples and applications of "time-tripping" are provided toward the end of this chapter.) The foregoing imagery excursion was then discussed, and Al was asked to practice similar scenes at his leisure several times a day, wherein he went back in time to comfort his young alter ego and upbraid his mother (assertively, not aggressively). In subsequent sessions, time-tripping was employed to encourage his (passive) father to stand up to his mother. Instead, the client preferred not to try to modify his father's behavior, but to inform him that from now on he (Al) was going to be a different (more assertive) individual. (It seemed that he was seeking permission to stop identifying with his father and to become his own person.) In my experience, when clients employ these imagery exercises conscientiously, salubrious effects usually accrue. Al was one of those clients who find these imagery exercises "ego-syntonic" and whose treatment gains coincide with their application. In tandem with the imagery exercises, each item on Al's Modality Profile was addressed. Thus, a nonperformance outlook on sex was underscored; approach responses rather than avoidance responses were encouraged; his anger, instead of being suppressed, was to be appropriately vented; relaxation skills were provided to offset his tension; images of positive erotic and sexual fantasies were to be practiced in place of his negative imagery; a strong antiperfectionistic philosophy of life was advocated; role playing was employed to enhance communication (e.g., stating sexual preferences explicitly); and behavior rehearsal was used to contend with criticism and aggression. The foregoing required *eight* weekly sessions, at the end of which time significant changes had accrued. (By the fifth session Al mentioned that during the. preceding week the sensate focus assignments had turned into "passionate love-making" on two occasions. Sensate focus procedures thus became their "new version of foreplay," and sexual intercourse occurred twice or three times a week thereafter.) Because Al still espoused certain sexual and marital myths, he was encouraged to reread Zilbergeld (1978) and pay particular attention to the myths outlined therein; I also gave him a copy of my book *Marital Myths* (Lazarus, 1985), suggesting that we might profitably discuss his reactions at the next session. One area that had not been specifically addressed was his ambivalence about parenthood, and it was recommended that we might focus on this issue during some further conjoint sessions.

Individual Sessions with Lisa. One of the significant features of the multi-modal approach is its flexibility. Lisa was negatively disposed to any systematic BASIC I.D. exploration but preferred to address the issues of self-blame and low self-esteem. Lisa's penchant for self-abnegation seemed to stimulate extremely defensive and overcompensatory (aggressive, hyper-critical) responses. The origin of her self-blame remained a mystery (she did not have the usual condemnatory, overcritical parents so often found in cases of this kind). Attempts to determine, through imagery, whether there were more subtle cues that had rendered her so vulnerable met with no success. Unlike Al, Lisa was unresponsive to mental imagery excursions. Consequently, the mainstay of therapy was focused on "cognitive restructuring," which endeavored to modify her dysfunctional beliefs.

Lisa was seen six times over a 9-week interval. In addition to cognitive therapy, her interpersonal style was a major focus for discussion in each of the meetings. It was impressed upon her that Al would probably always remain hypersensitive to actual or implied criticism, which he would tend to construe as an assault. I said, "I am trying to attenuate this sensitive zone, but I know of no method that will eliminate it." Role-playing was employed to teach Lisa an essentially supportive, nonpejorative, noncritical way of talking, disagreeing, arguing, questioning, and making requests. The virtues of positive reinforcement were underscored; when in doubt, she was counseled to fall back on the principle of positive connotation (i.e., to search for potentially caring, unselfish, and prosocial motives behind others' actions). "If you ever want to sabotage your marriage, just go ahead and criticize Al strongly, put him down as a man, and cast aspersions on his sexuality."

The sexual area per se required very little attention. Lisa stated that she was easily brought to orgasm, described herself as "sensual and uninhibited," and reported "no hang-ups in this area." She was cautioned again to beware of "coming on strong," of being critical, and of making demands instead of stating her preferences. I inquired, "Is this unfair? Are you being asked to do things or avoid things that are simply impossible in the long run?" "Not if I want this marriage to succeed," she answered.

Conjoint Sessions.   Three additional meetings with the couple consolidated their gains and also addressed the question of whether they should consider having a child. Al summarized it as follows: "I am still uncertain, but I think that's because I want guarantees. But I'm willing for us to stop using contraceptives for the next few months and see what happens."

Follow-Up.   Eleven months later, a follow-up inquiry revealed that Al and Lisa had maintained their gains and that Lisa was in the final weeks of pregnancy. Two years later I received a Christmas card with a photo of a smiling Al, Lisa, and their daughter with a note expressing thanks, explaining they had moved to the midwest, and adding "We're doing just fine."

Commentary.   While the treatment of Al and Lisa called for no heroic, extremely innovative, or especially intriguing tactics, it nevertheless illustrates quite well the relatively brief but comprehensive nature of the multimodal approach. A lot of territory was covered. The 2 conjoint intake sessions, the 8 individual sessions with Al, the 6 with Lisa, and the 3 final conjoint meetings add up to a total of 19 sessions The active educational emphasis (which will be elaborated on in Chapter 10) comes through clearly. Techniques were clearly matched to the predilections of the clients. Al resonated to imagery methods and found time-tripping most useful; Lisa was more "left brain"-inclined, and the use of imagery procedures was aborted. A pivotal dynamic seemed to revolve around the way in which Lisa's somewhat abrasive interpersonal style fed into Al's hypersensitivity to real or imagined criticism. In resolving this important clash-point, a good deal of territory was traversed during the 19 sessions, showing that brief but comprehensive therapy is not an oxymoron.

The comments about inhibited sexual desire and the case of Lisa and Al were excerpted from my chapter on problems of sexual desire in Leiblum and Rosen's (1988) book *Sexual Desire Disorders.*

MULTIMODAL TREATMENT OF DYSTHYMIA

Dysthymic Disorder

According to *DSM-IV,* people who suffer from dysthymic disorder display a depressed mood for most of the day, for more days than not, as indicated either by subjective account or observation by others, for at least 2 years.

They are never without depressive symptoms for more than 2 months at a time. The diagnosis calls for two (or more) of the following while depressed:

1. Poor appetite or overeating
2. Insomnia or hypersomnia
3. Low energy or fatigue
4. Low self-esteem
5. Poor concentration or difficulty making decisions
6. Feelings of hopelessness

Dysthymic individuals experience clinically significant distress or impairment in social, occupational, or other important areas of functioning. *DSM-IV* emphasizes the importance of determining that the symptoms are not due to the direct physiological effects of a substance (e.g., medication, or drug abuse) or to a general medical condition (e.g., hypothyroidism).

The typical entry point of a patient with a dysthymic disorder is his or her *affective* modality (i.e., complaints of sadness and unhappiness), coupled with *cognitive* problems (e.g., pessimism, negative self-statements, guilt, and an expressed lack of interest in activities that formerly were valued and enjoyed). There is, of course, no invariant sequence, and for some patients the se*nsory mode* is the entry point (i.e., they complain of somatic distress—aches, pains, and discomfort). Others may refer only to loss of libido, insomnia, reduced appetite, or diminished activity. Regardless, the multimodal clinician, after establishing rapport, endeavors to obtain sufficient information to list the salient problems across the BASIC I.D. Here is an example taken from the notes of a 36-year-old man:

- *Behavior:*   Reduced work performance, diminished activity, statements of self-denigration
- *Affect:*   Sadness, "heavy-hearted," intermittent anxiety
- *Sensation:*   Less pleasure from food and sex; easily fatigued
- *Imagery:*   Visions of loneliness and failure, pictures himself being rejected by important people in his life
- *Cognition:*   Negative self-appraisal, guilt; exaggerates real or imagined shortcomings
- *Interpersonal:*   Decreased social participation
- *Drugs/Biology:*   Intermittent insomnia

Many factors can contribute to this state of affairs. Obvious factors include loss of money, health, status, friendship, and loved ones. Less obvious circumstances may pertain to issues such as loss of youth, opportunity, novelty, or striving. It is important to identify specific reinforcement deficits.

Treatment

The essence of a successful treatment process is that people are enabled to recognize and utilize various positive reinforcers at their disposal. The multimodal orientation is predicated on the assumption that by treating only one or two significant problems or issues, relapse is likely. Thus, a depressed or dysthymic individual who is taught to dispute irrational ideas, and to identify a change in negative automatic thoughts, will remain vulnerable to future bouts of depression if behavioral deficits, sensory overloads, or negative imagery have not been identified and remedied. On the other hand, once these aspects have been ruled out, all that may be necessary is attention to cognitive dysfunctions, as will be discussed later in this chapter. In the interpersonal modality, lack of social skills and the presence of "family saboteurs" often call for explicit therapeutic attention. In this connection, it is interesting to note how "cognitive therapy" has become significantly broader and more eclectic over the years (Beck, 1991).

C. N. Lazarus (1991) compared standard psychiatric diagnoses (e.g., the *Diagnostic and Statistical Manual of Mental Disorders)* with multimodal assessment and problem identification (i.e., BASIC I.D. formulations). He addressed the heterogeneous range of depressive symptoms and showed that polar opposites are evident in several areas (e.g., insomnia vs. hypersomnia; psychomotor retardation vs. psychomotor agitation; weight gain vs. weight loss). He depicted two patients who presented with widely differing symptom clusters despite fully meeting the *DSM* criteria for depression. It was clear that from a clinical standpoint, the two depressed individuals required very different therapeutic regimens and the simple *DSM* label conveyed little clinically useful information. The multimodal assessment, on the other hand, yielded clear-cut problem clusters with sound treatment recommendations and precise clinical-decision-making strategies.

In treating dysthymic and other depressive disorders the following seven-pronged approach is recommended:

1: Behavior.   Many observers have found a correlation between high activity levels and the diminution of depressive affect. This is, of course, not a one-to-one relationship, for people can busy themselves with meaningless drudgery and become even more depressed despite an increase in activity per se. The emphasis, therefore, is on a catalog of rewarding activities. One proceeds to find out what activities had been rewarding in the past, and checklists are drawn up with the aid of a standard "pleasant events schedule." The aim is to establish numerous behaviors, sensations, images, ideas, people, and places that the client used to find rewarding. It is advisable to identify at least 20 items from which to work. Very simple, ordinary, everyday pleasures are sought (e.g., playing tennis, buying clothes, reading comics, playing cards, watching videos, telling jokes, taking a warm shower, engaging in sex, reliving pleasant scenes, listening to music, having a massage, eating in a good restaurant, talking on the telephone, taking walks, discussing religion, visiting friends, winning an argument, going to auctions, playing with pets.) Working from a list of activities that have once been rewarding, and probably still could be, enables the clinician to start recommending potentially reinforcing events. Those clients who do not respond readily to a mélange of reinforcements may require considerable attention and therapeutic interest and concern before engaging in activities that can begin to reverse the downhill trend that leads many to come for help. The habit of ensuring a daily sampling of personally pleasing activities is also an important way to prevent relapse. I recommend that my clients engage in at least a couple of simple "pleasure units" each day.

2: *Affect.*   Apart from differing degrees of misery and gloom, depressed patients often suffer from anxiety and anger. Whereas some dynamic theorists posit depression as "anger turned inward," close examination of the sources of various anger responses indicates that they are often secondary to the depression. It seems that significant others are placed in a difficult double bind when dealing with depressed persons. A display of warmth or sympathy, and any attempt to cheer them up, may serve only to aggravate the depressive reaction. The opposite response (withdrawal or nonreinforcement) may also augment the general sense of the patient's diminished self-worth, and result in (usually unexpressed) wrath and consequent guilt. Therapists' nonjudgmental acceptance often bypasses the foregoing processes and facilitates the opportunity to employ standard anxiety reduction methods (e.g., relaxation, meditation, calming self-statements), combined with assertiveness training (which tends to address both the anxiety and the anger components). The end product is a repertoire of self-assertive and uninhibited responses, which once again has both antidepressant effects and helps to diminish the likelihood of relapse.

3: *Sensation.*   In the sensory modality, a specific list of pleasant visual, auditory, tactile, olfactory, and gustatory stimuli is added to the aforementioned "pleasant events schedule." Moreover, exercises to promote muscle tone may be included in the regimen. In this regard, compliance with or adherence to treatment is not often easily achieved and usually requires considerable rapport and clinical artistry. When the patient becomes open to a "sensate focus" of enjoyable events, the treatment trajectory tends to be enhanced.

4: *Imagery.*   Patients who report an ability to conjure up vivid images (e.g., those who obtain high imagery score on the Structural Profile Inventory) have at their disposal a wide range of potentially powerful techniques. Among the most useful for overcoming depression are "recalling past successes," "picturing small but successful outcomes," "applying positive coping imagery," and using "time projection." Time projection has the patient picture him- or herself venturing step by step into a future characterized by positive affect and pleasurable activities. (This technique will be discussed at some length at the end of this chapter.) As a relevant aside, it is hoped that the reader can appreciate the degree of interdigitation among the modalities and their respective techniques. No specific rules pertain to the timing or ordering of the various multimodal procedures, and in the actual clinical situation, the selection and implementation of techniques is usually accomplished in concert with input from the patient.

5: *Cognition.*   In this modality, one of the principal objectives is to eliminate the non sequitur "therefore I am worthless." One parses irrational self-talk, challenges categorical imperatives and consequent standards that are impossibly high, and attends to other errors in the patient's depressive thinking such as dichotomous divisions, overgeneralization, negative expectations, and catastrophizing tendencies. Most cases of *bipolar depression* usually call for the therapist to commence with the "D" modality (i.e., prescribing lithium). In treating dysthymia, however, it is usually the cognitive modality that provides entry into treatment, soon followed by appropriate techniques drawn from one or more of the other six modalities. Clients who are willing to read recommended "popular" books find that they often serve as useful therapeutic adjuncts.

6: *Interpersonal Relationships.*   The patient's ability to deal with the demands of his or her significant network of people is the mainstay of treatment in this modality. Social skill deficits are identified and addressed; unassertive responses on the one hand, and aggressive reactions on the other, are delineated and replaced (whenever possible) by assertive behaviors. Role-playing is used quite extensively.

In essence, patients are taught four specific skills: (1) saying "no" to unreasonable requests; (2) asking for favors from others; (3) expressing positive feelings; and (4) volunteering criticism and disapproval "with style." Therapists well versed in assertiveness training often find that when patients learn to ask for what they want, resist unwelcome requests or exploitation from others, initiate conversations, and develop more intimate relationships, therapeutic gains are impressive. Nevertheless, the multimodal view is that unless significant problems throughout the BASIC I.D. are addressed, gains are likely to be short-lived. To the extent that interpersonal triggers can be identified (e.g., comments from a critical spouse), patients may be treated by desensitization, role-playing, and other familiar behavioral coping strategies.

7: *Drugs/Biology.* Biological intervention is often strongly advisable when dealing with bipolar disorders, or when the diagnosis is major depression; and even with dysthymic disorders, clinicians have found that many patients appear to derive benefits from antidepressants. In my experience, when patients spontaneously inquire about the possible advantages of medication, referral to a competent psychopharmacologist is usually effected after ensuring that the patient is not looking for a "magic bullet." Issues pertaining to increased exercise, relaxation, appropriate sleep patterns, and overall "physical fitness" are clearly addressed.

Application

In treating the 36-year-old man whose Modality Profile was outlined on page 89, three immediate interventions were selected. (1) His *diminished activity* and *decreased social participation* became the first target. In concert with input from the client, we discussed diversions, amusements, hobbies, forms of entertainment, and other pleasant events he could pursue instead of sitting and brooding. (2) His *statements of self-denigration* and his *negative self-appraisal* also received direct attention. His "mental filter," wherein he was apt to select only negative details to dwell on, totally disqualifying any positive experiences, was pointed out again and again. He was prompted to "adjust the scales" so that he developed a more balanced outlook. (3) His images of loneliness, failure, and rejection were offset by homework assignments wherein he was to focus on success images. He also required three sessions wherein he received formal desensitization to criticism and rejection.

At the seventh and final session he not only reported feeling significantly better but stated, "You won't believe this, but I'll be starting a new job next Thursday." In his case, a pervasive fear of rejection and failure had prevented him from taking any emotional risks. The impact of our sessions, he said, had rendered him relatively impervious to his former "bête noire—the deeply dreaded rejection!" He insisted that henceforth he would not become "cut up and unhinged" by rejection from women, his parents, or his employers. While this case was rather pedestrian, it is nevertheless noteworthy that a *trimodal* approach via behavior, cognition, and imagery rapidly effected some basic changes that will probably be maintained. At the end of therapy I always ask myself whether, as the old saying goes, I have merely given fish to my clients or whether I have taught them how to fish for themselves.

A Predominantly Cognitive Case of Dysthymia

The advantage of the multimodal assessment process is that it rapidly identifies the crucial dimensions that call for correction. As already stated, some people who suffer from dysthymic disorders are found to have significant behavioral deficits, and for them, the treatment trajectory needs to include a great deal of role-playing, modeling, coaching, and rehearsal. Similarly, if the clinical picture is characterized by sensory deficits, intrusive images, morbid daydreams, and a breadth of disturbing memories, it is highly advisable to address these issues and the modalities into which they fit. If the Multimodal Life History Inventory (Lazarus & Lazarus, 1991) and the initial interview do not reveal specific problems in particular areas, there is no point in dwelling on those topics, but there is every reason to zero in on the issues that do arise.

Dryden's *Brief Rational Emotive Behaviour Therapy* (1995) offers a wealth of cognitive and other specific techniques that can be employed both inside and outside therapy sessions. His section on clients' homework schedules and his checklist on possible reasons for not completing self-help assignments are most helpful. For example, to what extent do clients believe that if they follow the therapist's suggestions, it will hamper their own problem-solving skills? How many clients feel that the therapist is trying to control them by recommending specific homework assignments? And how many are apt to comply simply to earn the therapist's approval rather than to learn something useful for themselves? When issues of this kind emerge, they require attention before any specific methods can be implemented. When they are conspicuously absent, treatment can be rapid and effective.

Martin. By the end of the initial interview, it seemed clear that 40-year-old Martin displayed virtually all the common patterns of irrational thinking that many experts have cataloged. First, he was a *mind reader* and drew negatively toned inferences about the motives and thoughts of others. Martin *overgeneralized* by reaching unwarranted (negative) conclusions from small or minor events. He engaged in almost constant *all-or-none* thinking, where everything was stated in terms of polar extremes—"Either I'm a success or I'm a total failure." Martin also embraced a magnitude of *shoulds and musts*—imperatives for himself and others that rendered him vulnerable to resentment and guilt. His *negative predictions* reflected deep pessimism that led him to expect failure for all new situations and events. He was apt to *personalize*—to interpret situations and events in such a way that his negative self-appraisals were confirmed. He tended to *label* undesirable behaviors as immutable personality characteristics. Instead of saying, "I acted selfishly," he would declare, "I am a selfish person." He dismissed, disqualified, or ignored positive events and dwelled on real or imagined negative occurrences.

With so many dysfunctional cognitions in evidence, it seemed logical not to waste time drawing up Modality Profiles or administering tests, but to "go for the jugular" by addressing his many dysfunctional patterns of thinking. Dryden's caveats did not seem to apply, and so I immediately pointed out the patterns of irrational thinking he adopted, and inquired if he agreed that his outlook was colored by them. "I see what you're getting at," he replied, "but perhaps what I think about myself is real, not irrational." I answered: "You may be right. That's what we need to determine."

Martin was asked to recount various events, which he did in his typically despairing way. In every instance, I pointed out the necessity of testing alternative conceptualizations. For example, he reported that he had had a date the previous night that ended poorly.

MARTIN: I felt like an idiot. On the way back to her apartment it fell apart. We had, I can't say for sure, you know, but, you know, I'm pretty certain, actually, I, um, it's probably true that we sat in silence for 10 minutes. Yes, I would say that's about right, and that's, um, you know, like a very long time. And finally we parted company. Oh, boy!

THERAPIST: So are you saying that she came away thinking badly about you because you couldn't think of anything to say?

MARTIN: Right! I didn't say, I mean I ran out of steam. Can you just see it?

THERAPIST: Up to that point you had been pretty engaged, right?

MARTIN: Yeah, but when push came to shove, you know, my mind ended up turning to mush. I kept on, you know, like being frantic—frantically thinking that I must say something, must make conversation or something.

THERAPIST: How about the idea that two people are now enjoying their ride home, just sitting and relaxing, privately reflecting on the evening or just enjoying their own thoughts?

MARTIN: That's like great when you've been married for 10 years, but not on a first date!

THERAPIST: So in your eyes, this can be chalked up as yet another of your failures?

MARTIN: [Shrugs his shoulders] Uh huh.

THERAPIST: So she went inside thinking what? "Boy, oh boy, that Martin is such a jerk!"

MARTIN: Well, Maryann set up the date. "Why did you introduce me to that muttonhead?" You know, that's what she probably said to her. "He's a loser."

THERAPIST: Can you test out that hypothesis? Can you call Maryann and ask her what—what was her name?

MARTIN: Julie.

THERAPIST: Can you ask her what Julie actually reported?

At first, Martin was reluctant to expose himself to what he viewed as further ridicule. I pointed out that we needed to establish once and for all if his perceptions were accurate. If they did indeed turn out to be legitimate, therapy would be geared to correcting the dysfunctional patterns that occasioned his distress. "I would have to teach you how to stop being a muttonhead." However, if he was mistaken, and others did not view him in a negative light, therapy would be aimed at realigning his own perceptions. "I would have to teach you that you are not a muttonhead."

According to Maryann, Julie had liked Martin and had a pleasant evening. I pressed him to inquire from Maryann on what note Julie had thought the evening had ended. Her account was that after a rather hectic evening of dining, dancing, and conversation, they enjoyed a quiet drive back home while listening to the stereo.

I was able to persuade Martin to check the veracity of his negative perceptions by, whenever feasible, obtaining independent verification from others. "I want you to stop turning silver linings into clouds," he was told. At the same time, he was instructed to come up with what we called a Range of Alternatives (ROA). Thus, when he was not invited to join three of his associates for lunch, he concluded that they had rejected him because of their strong antipathy toward him. He was able to come up with the following ROAs:

1. They had something private among them to discuss that did not concern him.
2. Not asking him to join them was simply an oversight on their part.
3. They were on a Needs Assessment Committee and regarded it as a business lunch.

(It transpired that they were joggers who had decided to skip lunch and go for a run.)

At times, paradoxical remarks were used as a mirror to reflect Martin's self-downing tendencies:

MARTIN: My boss took a dim view of the fact that I was unable to find—what do you call it—the, um, sales figures from Merrill Lynch.

ME: What exactly did he say to you?

MARTIN: No, nothing. Um. It's just the way he looked.

ME: So you are mind-reading again. Okay, give me three ROAs.

MARTIN: [Pause] I can't think of any.

ME: Okay, I'll start you off with one. The Merrill Lynch statistics were not that important or else your boss would have insisted that you find them.

MARTIN: Oh, no, one of the secretaries told me what folder they were in, so I had them.

ME: Oh, I see. So it's back to the perfectionism game. Instead of whipping out the Merrill Lynch account in a flash, you hesitated, and one of the secretaries handed you the correct folder and on you went—or something like that?

MARTIN: Something like that.

ME: [Paradoxically] I know people who've been fired for less than that!

MARTIN: [Smiling] Okay, okay.

ME: How come they haven't fired a thick-skulled muttonhead like you ages ago?

MARTIN: [With a broad grin]. You've made your point.
ME: How can I get you to make these changes right inside you, where they count?
MARTIN: I'm getting there.

Martin was seen 15 times over 7 months. He was soon able to identify and acknowledge his irrational beliefs. He came to appreciate how these distorted ideas intruded into his views of himself and his relationships with others. He fully realized that his maladaptive beliefs were perpetuating unfortunate limitations on his personal dealings and were giving rise to painful emotions. He developed a risk-taking philosophy in which he habitually disconfirmed his negative cognitions by checking out his perceptions. It was particularly encouraging when he reported the following event at a follow-up interview (a year after therapy had terminated):

MARTIN: So I figured, well, you know, maybe Pete's attitude reflected, sort of, the fact that he, you know, saw me as too uptight to be part of his inner circle. I came up with two or three ROAs, and then I checked it out with him. Sure enough, you know, I was right to begin with, like it sort of all fitted in. He said that I did not fit in. That's what he said. "Well, you just don't fit in." He was right. For starters, they toss back three beers to my one. . . . So it's okay, you know, for some people to like me and for others to dislike me.
ME: Yeah, I guess everyone loves a clown because a clown doesn't stand for anything or threaten anyone. But when you're a man, a person with ideas, opinions, habits, and values, you can't and don't want to win them all.

The treatment process that Martin received underscores a point made by Bemporad (1995): "The type of psychotherapy should be tailored to the severity and form of the presenting depression . . . for ultimately, psychotherapy exerts its effects on the person, rather than on the disease" (p. 120).

NOTES ON TIME TRIPPING

As already mentioned, "time tripping" can be extremely useful. For example, a method I first called "Time Projection with Positive Reinforcement" (Lazarus, 1968) has proved successful with a number of people who became depressed after an annoying or distressing incident. Often, an event that caused intense irritation or sorrow can be viewed with indifference or detachment after, say, a lapse of 6 months or a year. This is probably because the passage of time permits new or competing responses to emerge (and that is why "time heals"). So what would happen if, in a single session, a patient vividly imagined going forward in time, day by day, week by week, while clearly visualizing enjoyable activities that he or she could engage in? When looking back at the distressing event from the vantage point of at least a 6-month imagined time lapse, would the individual then experience a diminution of negative affect? An affirmative answer has been obtained from a variety of people who were capable of actively immersing themselves in a sequence of positive imaginal events.

One of the first cases I reported was a 23-year-old woman who became acutely depressed when her boyfriend rejected her. A single time-projection session made a profound difference. She was asked to picture herself engaging in activities that she found especially rewarding—horseback riding, playing the guitar, painting, sculpturing, attending concerts, and being in the country. In the session, she was asked to dwell on these pleasant events one by one, to imagine herself actually enjoying them. Soon the days would start flying past; they would turn into weeks and then into months. She was asked to recount how many rewarding activities had been sampled. We dwelled on these pleasing events for a while, and then I said: "Now pretend that 6 real months have gone by. [Pause] How do you feel when you now reflect back to that incident that bothered you? It's now more than 6 months old." She stated: "How can I put it in words? Let me just explain it in three ways. First, I feel kind of foolish; second, there are lots of pebbles on the beach; and number three, there's something inside that really wants to find an outlet on canvas. Does that make sense?" A week later, the client reported that her appetite had returned, she was sleeping well again, and she had enjoyed many productive hours. Thereafter she continued making satisfactory progress.

Future time-projection using images of positive reinforcement is no cure for deep-seated depression. But it has shown itself to be a rapid and lasting means for helping people with minor depressions who otherwise might very well have remained needlessly unhappy and distressed for considerable periods of time. Scores of people who suffered minor depressions over specific events have been helped by this time projection technique.

There are also many instances when it is expedient to travel back in time. For example, many clients carry grudges or otherwise remain affected by past hurts and indignities. When these individuals remain unresponsive to the usual therapeutic procedures—cognitive disputation and reframing, discussion and ventilation, formal desensitization, and so forth—time tripping into the past is often effective (again, though, only with people who are responsive to imagery procedures).

Thus, a 25-year-old man was extremely distressed about an event that occurred at his eighth birthday party. Time tripping was employed as follows: "Try to imagine that we have a time machine and that you can travel back in time. You enter the time machine, and within a few moments you have gone back to that incident when you were unfairly punished in front of strangers. As you step out of the time machine, you are your present age, and you see your alter ego, yourself at age 8. Can you imagine that?" The client answered affirmatively, and the time tripping continued: "The 8-year-old senses something special about this adult man who has just entered the picture. He doesn't realize, of course, that you are that same little boy, all grown up, out of the future. Nonetheless, he will pay close attention to you. You can really get through to him."

The time-tripping procedure then had the client reassuring his alter ego, while providing succor, support, understanding, and an explanation of the intentions behind the perpetrator's (his father's) misguided actions. The client was then asked to step back into the time machine and return to the present so that we could analyze and review the impact of his excursion. This method often yields a rapid cognitive reframing of and desensitization to unpleasant memories.

I described one seemingly intractable case, a 32-year-old woman who conjured up image after image, retrieved "forgotten memories," instituted a series of "court scenes" against her offenders, and introduced several other novel ways of coming to terms with past agonies—a process that extended over 7 months of weekly sessions—before finally declaring, "I have worked all that out of my system" (Lazarus, 1989b). In most instances, time tripping, either into the future or back to the past, is a rapid means of dispelling various forms of emotional distress.

CHAPTER 10

Couples Therapy

In chapter 9, a couples therapy case was presented that dealt primarily with sexual desire disorders. In the present chapter we will consider a broader range of issues pertaining to conjoint therapy.

Couples therapy is not a unified form of treatment but draws on a heterogeneous range of influencing processes. When individual agendas, hidden or other, undermine a relationship, individual therapy is often essential before the couple can benefit from conjoint therapy. When distressed couples are relatively stable and are genuinely interested in achieving a harmonious relationship, salubrious outcomes can usually be achieved in six or seven sessions of "didactic instruction"(Lazarus, 1992). In this regard, the main emphasis is on encouraging the couple to abandon coercive tactics, to forgo impossible romantic ideals, to appreciate the value of reciprocity, to put commonsense do's and don'ts into effect, and to replace negative impasses with constructive compromises and negotiations. In these cases, a few "training sessions"can equip them to apply good listening skills, to use positive communication styles, apply *quid pro quo* interactions, and employ positive reinforcement.

USEFUL TECHNIQUES

To expedite matters, one should not shy away from using simple but effective procedures. For example, I find it useful to discuss each item of the following "Seven Basic Ground Rules," handing out three copies—one for her purse, another for his wallet, and a third for their refrigerator door:

1. Never criticize a person; ask for a specific change in his or her behavior.
2. Don't mind-rape (i.e., do not tell the other person what he or she is thinking or feeling).
3. Avoid saying, "You always . . ." or "You never . . ." Be specific.
4. Avoid right-wrong, good-bad categories. When differences arise, look for compromises.
5. Use "I feel" messages instead of "You are" messages. For example, say, "I feel hurt when you ignore me!" but do not say, "You are selfish and inconsiderate for ignoring me."
6. Be direct and honest. Say what you mean and mean what you say.
7. I'm okay, you're okay. I count, you count.

In cases, however, where one or both partners harbor accumulated resentments, suffer from undue anxiety, or display abject misery or extreme insecurity, therapy is apt to follow a more tortuous pathway. The same is true for those couples whose dyadic distress is occasioned by pernicious demands, distorted perceptions, or clear-cut psychopathology.

Within the first two sessions, the therapist should be able to determine if there is (1) genuine love and caring, (2) a viable level of emotional stability, and (3) no evidence of gross incompatibility. When conditions (1) and (3) do not apply, divorce counseling becomes a logical alternative. If (1) and (3) apply but (2) does not (i.e., one or both are psychologically disturbed), in most instances therapy needs to be directed at the individuals and their disorders. Contrary to those system theorists who insist on working only within dyadic, triadic, or family contexts, it is my experience that in the aforementioned circumstances, individual therapy needs to be the major vehicle of change (Lazarus, 1992). Ellis (1962) stated:

> If neurotics have basically irrational assumptions or value systems, and if these assumptions lead them to interact self-defeatingly with their mates, then the marriage counselor's function is to tackle not the problem of the marriage, nor of the neurotic interaction that exists between the marital partners, but of the irrational ideas or beliefs that cause this neurosis à deux." (p. 210)

With couples who seem to be in a rut, I will typically use the Triple-Increase Technique, even in the very first session. Each partner is asked for a list of three specific behaviors he or she would like the other partner to *increase*. It is explained that asking for change in terms of increases rather than decreases is apt to be positive rather than pejorative. "I wish you'd stop biting your nails so your hands wouldn't look so ugly, " versus "I wish you'd increase the length of your nails so your hands would look more attractive."

When compiling their lists, most people usually are too vague and general. "I'd like her to increase her level of affection." "I'd like him to increase his caring and concern." They are told that nebulous statements need to be replaced by highly *specific behaviors.* "Instead of chatting for 5 or 6 minutes after dinner, I'd like us to increase the time to 15 or 20 minutes." If the partners are unable to come up with three specific requests each during the session, they are asked to complete the assignment before the next session and to bring their lists with them. Noncompliance, of course, becomes grist for the mill.

Here are lists from one of the couples who sought therapy:

I want Carol to increase:
(1) The number of times she visits my parents.
(2) The number of times a week she is willing to make love.
(3) The number of times she cooks in rather than sends out for dinner.

I want Michael to increase:
(1) The number of days he gets back from the office before 7 P.M.
(2) The occasions when he spontaneously unloads the dishwasher and takes out the garbage (without having to be reminded).
(3) The number of times he compliments me.

The therapist discusses each item and inquires if it is acceptable to the other partner. If not, the items have to be modified. When the couple agrees that the requests are reasonable, the focus shifts to the implementation of each item. In the foregoing case, Michael would be asked to state how many days a week he will be home before 7 P.M. and how often he will attend to the requested chores. The therapist notes this down on a Pledge Sheet: "Michael agrees to be home before 7 P.M. at least twice a week." Sometimes couples prefer to make trade-offs. "I agree to cook dinner on those nights I know you will be home before 7 P.M." When the negotiations are done, each partner signs his or her Pledge Sheet. The main point about this method is that it provides six important behaviors that get written into the marital script, thus generally increasing overall levels of satisfaction.

One can often be more directive and zoom into issues more rapidly when working with couples than with individuals. Unless the couple is almost literally at each other's throat, there tends to be a two-against-one component (husband and wife are apt to team up) where, if the therapist comes on too strong, one or both members of the dyad tend to say or do something to rescue the other.

ASSESSING THE COUPLE

One of the first factors to assess is if both partners genuinely want to improve their relationship, or if one or both have entered "couples therapy" with the predetermined intention of obtaining a divorce. In the latter case, perhaps they can be helped to achieve a reasonably amicable uncoupling process. As already stated, it is also important to assess if a dyadic or individual focus is advisable. For example, a woman who suffered from agoraphobia made incessant demands on her husband. She kept calling him for reassurance when he was at the office and would not let him out of her sight when they were together. "She's driving me nuts!" he complained. Here, individual therapy with the wife, employing a robust combination of cognitive and behavioral interventions, significantly attenuated her phobic reactions in 11 sessions. Contrary to some theorists who would think otherwise, profoundly positive changes accrued that have endured 4 years, despite the fact that the couple's marital transactions were ignored and the husband was not involved in the treatment (apart from escorting his wife on some planned in vivo excursions).

Similarly, with another couple, when it seemed evident that the major source of marital tensions was the fact that the husband was clinically depressed, he was referred to a psychiatrist for medication while I also worked with him individually, mainly employing "cognitive therapy." After seven sessions over a 2- month interval, substantial progress had been achieved. I have seen therapists who continued to treat couples who, from my perspective, were bound to remain impervious to their ministrations unless and until certain individual impediments could be overcome.

A TYPICAL SEQUENCE

Ordinarily after writing down formal details such as the names, address, telephone numbers, ages, occupations, duration of marriage, children (if any), and so forth, I will usually say, "What seems to be the problem? " It is interesting that with many couples, there is a "defendant" and a "complainant" (putting it in legalistic terms). Madge remonstrates, "Our main fights have to do with the fact that Charlie refuses to help around the house and he never disciplines the children, so that I end up being the heavy." Charlie, entering a plea in his own defense states, "Don't I help you with the dishes, and didn't I tell Cindy to be home by 11 P.M.?" Madge responds, "Big deal! One swallow doesn't make a summer. The point is that apart from occasionally helping with the dishes you do absolutely nothing around the house, and most times you leave it to me to correct Cindy and Mike. "

The aim is to identify key issues that create confusion, cause dissension and distress, and otherwise undermine a couple's contentment. In this connection, I make use of the standard Multimodal Life History Inventory when it seems advisable to fathom one or both partners in much greater depth and detail; but in most instances the Expanded Structural Profile (see Appendix 3) is used with couples. It immediately brings to light contrasts and comparisons that permit one to identify and focus on significant differences and important similarities. For example, upon studying his wife's answers on the Profile, a husband stated: "It shows me to what extent I'm more of a loner while she's definitely a people person. So whereas I would like to decrease the large family get-togethers, she wants more of them. And it confirms that she's a thinker or a planner while I fly by the seat of my pants, which sometimes irritates her no end." These comments of specified divergence led to a constructive plan that permitted the couple to appreciate their differences when making various plans and decisions.

Note that the major emphasis is on identifying processes and reactions that can prove of immediate help in cementing a better relationship. Examining too many "underlying issues" usually leads to conceptual and clinical dead ends.

USING THE MARITAL SATISFACTION QUESTIONNAIRE

After listening to some of the bones of contention and noting the style that each partner adopts, I may ask the couple to fill out the Marital Satisfaction Questionnaire (see Appendix 4). The reliability and validity of this inventory was demonstrated by Herman (1991a).

When examining the questionnaire, it is more illuminating to discuss scores on individual items than to dwell on quantitative findings (although low overall totals will alert one to the degree of dissatisfaction that prevails). For example, when discussing low scores on item 2, "I am pleased with the *quality* of our communication," issues pertaining to *fear of intimacy* often emerge and can become pivotal to the treatment process. It is also helpful to examine the importance of any discrepancies between self-rated levels of satisfaction and the partner's estimates. For example, referring to Madge and Charlie again, she had given herself a high satisfaction rating on the item, "I am satisfied with the way we are spending/managing money," but she assumed that Charlie would express strong dissatisfaction in that regard. In fact, his score also reflected high satisfaction with their money management. "That amazes me," Madge asserted, "because Charlie is always accusing me of spending too much money on my exercise classes." "My only objection," Charlie explained, "is that I regard having a personal trainer as a waste of money. In general, I see you as a very good money manager and I trust you completely." Specific dialogues about various items tend to clear up many misunderstandings.

The Marital Satisfaction Questionnaire simply taps into the major areas of concern that most couples report—communication, sex, money, togetherness, friendships, parenting, family relationships, trust, values, and personal habits. It is interesting how a simple question about a specific rating can point to crucial interactions. For example, with a couple who both reported high overall satisfaction scores and who accurately predicted each others' specific ratings, one item stood out. The husband had given his wife "2" on item 12: "I am able to trust what my spouse/partner says and does." When asked to what this low rating referred, the husband spoke, with great emotion, about his wife's past infidelities—a topic that had eluded other avenues of inquiry. This turned out to be a pivotal issue that the couple tended to shelve and avoid discussing. It resulted in a most productive interchange.

Here is an additional example:

THERAPIST: Madge, you rated the item "I am of the opinion that my spouse is on my team" kind of low. You gave it a 3. Can you elaborate for me, please?

WIFE: I dunno. I, well, it's sort of about his habit of walking out of the room, especially if I mention any, kind of, problems. It also sort of ties into the whole thing about affection. He's not very affectionate, you know.

HUSBAND: That's not what is meant by "being on one's team."

THERAPIST: Well, let's hear what Madge is telling us. Is it true that you often withdraw from her when she wants to talk . . . ?

WIFE: [Interrupting] Especially when I want to talk about our relationship. Or if I have any negative feelings I want to share. That's when he cuts out.

HUSBAND:	Madge, you often pick the dandiest times to bring up matters for discussion. [Turns to face the therapist] I mean I've just walked in the door. I've had a hell of a day at work and, boom, she hits me with a complaint.
WIFE:	That's not true! But there never is a good time as far as you are concerned.
THERAPIST:	Wait a moment. [Turning to husband] Charlie, the point that Madge seems to be making is that she does not feel you are affectionate and she wonders how much you care for her. [Turning to wife] Is that right?
HUSBAND:	That's ridiculous.
THERAPIST:	Meaning that you do love her and care for her?
HUSBAND:	Absolutely. [Turning to wife] How can you doubt that?
WIFE:	[Starts to cry]
THERAPIST:	What do the tears signify, Madge?
WIFE:	[Blowing her nose] It just feels so good to be reassured.
THERAPIST:	Okay, so we're on to something. She feels your actions belie your words, Charlie, so how can you prove to her that you mean what you say?
WIFE:	Most of the time we are on the same team, but if only Charlie wouldn't give me the brush-off when I want to discuss a problem.

The foregoing interaction led naturally to my recommending a powerful technique—Time-limited Intercommunication—that has proved especially helpful with many clients who were willing to use it regularly.

TIME-LIMITED INTERCOMMUNICATION

The partners are asked to set aside two (three if possible) half-hour long appointments with each other every week for the next month. Five things are necessary—a quiet room where they will not be interrupted, an automatic timer, pencil, paper, and a coin.

The coin is flipped to determine who talks first. The timer is set for 5 minutes. During the first 5-minute interval, the talker discusses whatsoever she or he pleases. *The listener may not interrupt.* He or she may take notes in preparation for clarification or rebuttal, but no verbal output is to occur until the 5 minutes have elapsed and the timer goes off (unless the talker does not require the full five minutes and says "I'm through for now").

When the timer goes off, the talker is to stop speaking immediately. At that point, the listener paraphrases the speaker's message. If the speaker is not satisfied with the listener's feedback, she or he says, "You haven't got it quite right," and proceeds to explain what the listener misheard or where he or she went wrong. The listener paraphrases again and again until the talker is satisfied and feels properly heard and fully understood. The timer is then set for another 5 minutes, with the previous listener now doing the talking under the same ground rules.

In a typical half-hour session, each person usually gets two separate 5-minute opportunities to speak. If the paraphrases are brief and accurate, couples may take a few extra minutes and each have three talking and listening periods. At the end of the session the partners are instructed to hug each other and to drop any further discussion of the issues that were raised until the next preset appointment.

Some couples prefer hour-long time-limited intercommunications and have the patience and stamina to endure them. One purpose of making these dialogues *time-limited* is to avoid lengthy nit-picking debates. After putting this process into effect, couples typically report that they manage to cover all the important ground in less time. A few 3-minute "speeches" followed by 30-second paraphrases may then suffice to keep open the channels of communication.

Even when things are going well, some couples report that they use this technique once or twice a month to get matters off their chest and to ensure that no issues are festering *sub rosa.*

Bibliotherapy has also proved to be exceedingly helpful with many couples. When I see people who espouse some of the myths discussed in my book on *Marital Myths* (Lazarus, 1985), I give them a copy and ask them to read selected points for discussion (e.g., if they entertain false romantic beliefs, believe in quintessential togetherness, see marriage as a forum to "let it all hang out," and feel compelled to transform the spouse into a "better person"). This generally facilitates and expedites the course of treatment. Using bibliotherapy with couples often stimulates rapid change. The didactic and collaborative nature of such reading assignments triggers the sharing of ideas, diminishes relationship-defeating beliefs, and reduces the defensive and adversarial postures that distressed couples typically display.

OTHER TECHNIQUES

The technically eclectic outlook outlined in chapter 4 encourages one to draw on methods from a variety of approaches. For example, when couples seem to be hiding their feelings, it often helps to adapt and apply the "doubling" method from psychodrama, wherein the therapist expresses the presumed hidden content of a patient's feelings. The excerpt below is taken from Lazarus (1996). In this case, the husband was reluctant to ask his wife for more time and attention which, during individual sessions, he had said he wanted. The usual assertiveness training methods were proving ineffective. Consequently, I decided to test the technique of the *double,* which endeavors to express and clarify a patient's unspoken thoughts. I stood behind the husband and requested that he ask his wife to schedule more time together over weekends. After a few false starts, the following ensued:

HUSBAND:	"Do you think it might be good to make plans to do some things together on Saturdays and Sundays?"
ME:	[standing behind him and talking for him] "It really would mean a lot to me. It might make me feel that you still care for me."
WIFE:	[responding to my statement] "Is that true? I mean is that right? You think I no longer have feelings for you?"
HUSBAND:	"Uh. I wouldn't say that. Not really."
ME:	"Frankly my dear, I don't know what has happened to most of the good feelings that first attracted us to each other."
HUSBAND:	"Well, I think that's going too far."
ME:	[still doubling] "I find it too painful to acknowledge the fact that we have grown apart in many respects."
WIFE:	[addressing me] "I think you're exaggerating the situation."
ME:	[repositioning myself behind the wife's chair] "I find it easier to bury myself in my work and hang out with my sister than face the fact that we are drifting apart."
WIFE:	[addressing her husband] "Didn't you tell me that you need to spend time by yourself?"
HUSBAND:	"That's right. I wouldn't want a woman who was constantly on my back or in my hair."
ME:	[positioning myself behind the husband again] "But I think we have too much independence—much more than is good for us."
WIFE:	"When I suggested that we could both take tennis lessons together, you vetoed the idea."
ME:	"Well, doing *things* together is less important to me than knowing that you genuinely choose to be with me, that you really want to be in my company."

WIFE: [emotionally] "You've not made me feel that you exactly value *my* company."

HUSBAND: "How have I managed to convey that impression?"

WIFE: "How often do you tell me that you're fed up with people and would like to run off to some island?"

ME: [no longer doubling but addressing the husband] "Did you leave out three words—*together with you?*"

HUSBAND: "She knows I'd hate to live by myself."

ME: "She knows nothing of the sort." [Addressing the wife] "Am I correct?"

WIFE: [nods at me, turns to her husband] "Honey, I think he's got a point. We do tend to take each other and too many things for granted."

After this brief detour, therapy became firmly grounded once more in well-established behavioral methods—homework assignments, contingency contracts, behavior rehearsal, and skills training. The point of this vignette is to demonstrate the virtues of technical eclecticism. When basic behavioral techniques failed to achieve their desired effects, borrowing a method from a different discipline enabled this couple to hear each other clearly, thereby cutting to the core of what was most distressing for them. However, it would be an egregious error to claim that I was practicing "psychodrama" in this example. I had merely adapted a technique from psychodrama and had used it within my own (very different) framework (see Lazarus, 1996, and Appendix 5).

ADDITIONAL POINTS OF EMPHASIS

A "Magic Ratio"

Gottman (1994), on the basis of extensive research, has come up with what he terms a "magic ratio" of 5 to 1: "As long as there is five times as much positive feeling and interaction between husband and wife as there is negative, we found the marriage was likely to be stable" (p. 57). He also confirms a view espoused many years ago by Bach and Wyden (1969)—that intense arguments and the airing of complaints and grievances can signal highly effective adjustments, depending on how the couple fights. Dirty fighting—character assassination, personal criticism, dredging up the past, accusing, blaming, threatening, issuing ultimatums, and resorting to any of the 54 "relationship traps" discussed by Fay (1994)—will be bound to undermine and destroy the love and trust that characterize an effective relationship.

Saying "No!"

Fay (1994) points out that in intimate relationships, saying "No" "can be deadly " (p. 58). I agree. Saying "No" or refusing requests is perhaps one of the most destructive and pernicious habits. Interestingly, books on assertiveness training encourage people to stand up for their rights and not to say "Yes" when they want to say "No"—and not to feel guilty about saying "No." This is sage advice for dealing with pesky and pushy sales-people, or when employers attempt to take unfair advantage, or when manipulative and exploitive people attempt to exert unfair control. With intimates, it makes sense to say "Yes" unless there is a valid reason to say something else. Thus, in answer to the question, "Darling, will you do me a favor?" the best response is "Sure. What is it you want me to do? " To say, "Leave me alone; I'm busy," or "Stop bugging me," or any other variant of "No," hardly endears one to the other person or enhances the relation-ship. To say, "It depends on the favor," is not as negative as the foregoing, but an unqualified "Yes" is best. If necessary, one can negotiate matters if the request seems unreasonable, or if other commitments get in the way. "I'm quite willing for your mother to stay with us for 3 or 4 weeks, but hav-ing her here for over 6 weeks seems a bit much." "Ordinarily, I'd be delighted to drive Jake to see his math tutor, but I'm meeting with two out-of-town buyers and won't be home in time."

Here is a typical incident. A couple was very distressed over an event involving a 16-year-old daughter who was dating the quarterback of the high school football team. An important practice match was scheduled for 6 P.M. The daughter very much wanted to go to the practice and suggested that she would grab a bite to eat at 5.30. "Nothing doing," her father said. "You will sit down to dinner with the rest of the family at the usual time." This led only to an argument which created family strife and turmoil and cul-minated in the daughter's leaving the house, greatly upset, without having anything to eat. I asked the father why he had not gone along with his daughter's request. He said that the dinner hour was an important time for family togetherness and that he preferred sitting down to a meal with every-one present. "I can understand that," I said, "but it seems advisable to be flexible." I went on to say that it is not difficult to comprehend why it was so important for his daughter to attend the event, and how much better off everyone would have been had he not stood in her way. "In retrospect, " he conceded, "I agree with that."

The wife then proceeded to describe her husband as resorting to an automatic "No" far too often. "Most times," she said, "when the kids or I ask him for something the first answer out of his mouth is 'no,' but then he may think it over and change his mind." I pointed out that this is better than those no-sayers who feel they must "stick to their guns," even when they realize that they are being arbitrary and capricious. Nevertheless, I strongly encouraged the husband to think twice before saying "No."

Analogies and Metaphors

The following analogies and metaphors seem to facilitate a better balance in a relationship.

Marriage is like a finely balanced two-person sailboat. If one person moves way to the right, the other will have to quickly move to the left to balance the boat. If either one punches a hole in the boat, it will soon start sinking unless repairs are rapidly executed.

Thus, when a husband directed a harsh expletive at his wife in one of our sessions, I immediately said, "You've just put a rather large hole in the boat. If your intent is to sink it, do nothing. If you wish to remain afloat, let's quickly discuss ways and means of effecting repairs." He grew contrite and we discussed the issue from several angles and arrived at a suitable *modus vivendi.*

With a different couple, the wife—a psychologist—accused her husband of being passive-aggressive and of setting her up to be "the ogre and the heavy with the children." That very morning, their 7-year-old daughter had asked for help with homework she was supposed to have done before going to bed. This resulted in an argument with the mother, and the child ended up missing the school bus. The mother refused to drive her to school and insisted that she ride her bicycle; this escalated matters, and the father ended up driving her to school. "That's what I mean," the wife explained, "he undermined my authority and made me out to be the bad guy." She added that in her estimation he tended to behave in this way to get back at her for some unexpressed resentment. "The point of the matter, " the husband said, "was that she did not handle the situation calmly but got all bent out of shape, yelled at the kid, and, as usual, they fed into one another." He went on to explain that had his wife, instead of arguing with the child, gently discussed the situation, perhaps informing the child that after school they would need to sit down and discuss a better plan for the future, the kid would have been on time for the bus. "Under the circumstances," he added, "I thought she was too upset to ride her bike safely, so it made sense for me to drive her."

Using the sailboat analogy, I said that it seemed that the mother had veered rather far to one side, thereby forcing her husband to shift to the opposite end to keep the craft level. Rather pensively, the wife said, "So it's not a setup," and added, "I see how I can reframe it , which sure makes me see things differently."

A different metaphor, provided by Karpel (1994), is also often helpful. He compares a couple to "two individuals, each standing on a small raft, being carried along by the current of a river . . . each is balancing on his or her own raft and balancing across rafts with one another . . . The individuals try to maintain the connection, to take the dips and jolts [in the river] in tandem" (p. 1). Karpel's metaphor shows the necessity of attending simultaneously to the couple's relationship and to the individual partners. The reader who is interested in using metaphors in therapy is referred to Kopp's interesting book, *Metaphor Therapy* (1995).

When treating couples, clinicians place themselves in jeopardy if they develop a strong desire to save the relationship. While I was listening to the tape of one of my supervisees treating a couple, I carefully noted an interaction where the husband angrily said that perhaps divorce was their best option, whereupon the trainee launched into an impassioned plea to consider their young children. The wife responded by saying that if the only reason for preserving the marriage was for the sake of the children, there was little point in continuing. My trainee proceeded to dig herself into a deeper and deeper hole.

I recommended that my supervisee, at the next session, commence by pointing out to the couple that she had allowed sentiment to get in the way of good judgment. Upon rethinking matters and after discussing it with her supervisor, she now fully agreed that if there was insufficient love and caring, divorce was possibly a sensible option—children or no children. She conveyed this message, and both husband and wife thereupon stated, quite emphatically, that there was indeed a large pool of mutual affection and that they would like their marriage to succeed.

On many occasions, when couples have started feuding and clashing in my consulting room, I have blandly stated that perhaps we ought to consider working toward an amicable divorce. This usually shocks the couple into working together productively. On other occasions, when divorce counseling became the desired trajectory, I found it helpful to perform this function—despite the fact that we had apparently started out trying to save the marriage. Many people have claimed that it is inadvisable, and perhaps unethical, for a therapist who first served as a marriage counselor to then assume the role of divorce mediator. I disagree. I have found that having established mutual trust with the couple, I am often in a good position to mediate a fair if not amiable divorce. Of course, there have been occasions on which matters escalated and the services of someone well versed in legal technicalities were required.

One does not have to be sickly-sentimental to derive enormous gratification from transforming a dysfunctional couple into a harmonious dyad. A well-functioning marriage is a joy to behold.

CHAPTER 11

Some Common Time Wasters

Brief therapy is about using time efficiently, sensibly, pragmatically, and effectively. Clinicians who had been trained in and embraced a long-term focus and who, given the exigencies of our era, have recently converted to brief therapy, tend to remain exceedingly good at wasting time.

For example, a couple I had been seeing rapidly resolved their own marital difficulties, but considerable tension between them and their adult children remained a bone of contention. Their children were all high-level professionals, married, with no untoward difficulties in their own marriages and nuclear families. They lived out of state, and whenever their parents called or paid them a visit, I would hear (from my clients, the parents) that a certain degree of discomfort that had arisen. As is my custom, I wrote letters to their children asking for an outline of the issues that generated tension between them and their parents. I received no reply and was told by my clients that I was regarded as their (the parents') agent and could therefore not remain objective. The children arranged for a series of therapy sessions close to their homes with a family therapist who saw them together with their parents. After about five sessions the father declared it "a waste of time." His wife was more charitable and felt that some good had come out of the meetings but could not describe any specific gains. When the family therapist suggested several meetings with the parents to delve into their respective family backgrounds, the father became irritated and disillusioned. I did not wish to prejudice matters but inwardly agreed with his appraisal that this would be another waste of time. The father said, "I think we need to understand what is happening now and we need to find a way of communicating a lot better in the near future." Matters improved after the family therapist and I had a long telephone conversation and discussed several active strategies for achieving the aforementioned objectives.

A different kind of time waster is the belief that some therapists embrace about needing to delve into the nuances of the patient-therapist relationship. When progress is evident and therapy is proceeding apace, what is the point of this exercise? In the vast majority of cases, I end up without having the vaguest idea of how or what my clients *really* feel about me. I would assume that they were positively disposed by virtue of the fact that they were polite, respectful, friendly, and cooperative and usually seemed satisfied with their gains. However, when difficulties arose, when therapy stalled, and when progress faltered, one of the hypotheses I would entertain is that a problem between client and therapist may have arisen. What Safran refers to as ruptures in the therapeutic alliance justify investigation (Safran, Crocker, McMain, & Murray, 1990). But I repeat, if therapy is going well, gains are accruing, and progress is evident, why waste time analyzing the so-called "transference?"

Another time waster occurs when a client is able, willing, and ready to change but ends up in the hands of a therapist who employs only nondirective and supportive methods. Howard, Nance, and Myers (1987) discussed appropriate and inappropriate therapist styles for various levels of *readiness* and explicated a range of optimal and suboptimal procedures. Their work predates Prochaska and DiClemente's (1992) transtheoretical approach, which emphasizes five stages of change—precontemplation, contemplation, preparation, action, and maintenance. We touched on these notions in chapter 1. Basically, some clients are merely "window shoppers" who will be abashed by pushy or aggressive salespeople; others are considering a purchase but are still uncertain; and there are shoppers who are definitely readying themselves for an expenditure in the very near future. The action-oriented buyers arrive with cash on hand and expect to make a purchase. These people are unlikely to take kindly to anyone who recommends additional contemplation and cogitation.

Thus, one of my clients, a fifth-grade schoolteacher with a history of two unsuccessful marriages involving physical abuse, realized that she suffered from a fundamental lack of assertiveness which resulted in undue exploitation from others. After reading a book on assertive women, she consulted a therapist with the expectation that she would be taught some essential skills. Unfortunately for her, the doctor she consulted happened to practice only deep exploratory methods. The client was too unassertive to express her discontent but instead continued seeing the doctor, who analyzed her dreams and discussed her family background. Finally, a friend persuaded her to seek treatment elsewhere, and she was referred to me by the Cognitive Therapy Center in Philadelphia.

It has long been understood that people enter therapy with certain expectations, and that the effectiveness of the therapy is closely linked with these expectations. As a schoolteacher, the client resonated very well with my explanations about approaching therapy as a form of education; and as she was more than ready for change, she entered into the role-playing and behavior-rehearsal techniques of assertiveness training with alacrity. We discussed a general TNC (Take No Crap) outlook on life which the client was very eager to implement. After three sessions she recounted several instances of assertive behaviors in circumstances where she had normally been timid and submissive. After the fourth session we agreed to terminate therapy, although she was free to return for booster sessions if needed. She never looked back, and after 2 years called to say that she was remarried, adding that she continued to live up to the TNC philosophy.

Note that the multimodal orientation calls for flexibility. There is no slavish adherence to any protocol. In this case, no Multimodal Life History Inventory seemed necessary, and no BASIC I.D. schema was employed—instead, the most obvious issues were addressed head-on. Why waste time?

Yet another egregious time waster is the concept of a panacea. "Panacea pundits" tout and believe in the universal efficacy of a specific method or procedure. This harks back to the unfortunate "one size fits all" mentality. I know of clinicians who hook every one of their clients up to biofeedback machines, despite the fact that it has long been known that some people have untoward reactions to biofeedback procedures (Miller & Dworkin, 1977). There are those who glorify the presumed quintessential virtues of meditation, notwithstanding the fact that adverse reactions render some clients unsuitable candidates (e.g., Kennedy, 1976; Lazarus, 1976a). But perhaps the method that has been most widely promoted as a universal stress reducer is *deep muscle relaxation*. There is no book on stress reduction that I have seen which does not emphasize the widespread virtues of relaxation training. I have served on panels with Herbert Benson of Harvard University, who is an ardent promoter of what he calls the "relaxation response." And yet, many reports of RIA—*relaxation-induced-anxiety*—have appeared in the literature (e.g., Heide & Borkovec, 1983, 1984; Lazarus &

Mayne, 1990). The efficient use of therapeutic time calls for an immediate shift away from any procedure or process that is not promoting the anticipated well-being. One cannot overemphasize the need for clinicians to have at their disposal a wide range of effective techniques. Thus, if relaxation training seems to evoke disturbing reactions, one may gracefully switch to meditation. If this also proves ineffective or disturbing, a variety of imagery and visualization methods may be tried.

I am fond of pointing out that strawberry farmers may encourage us to consume lots of strawberries. "They are good for you. They are low in calories, high in fiber, and contain health promoting vitamins and minerals." Well and good, except if one happens to be allergic to strawberries! Indeed, clients may be "allergic" to a wide variety of psychological interventions, and it behooves therapists to avoid inducing psychic anaphylaxis.

A common time waster that I have referred to in several parts of this book is the notion that it is inadvisable for a therapist to take action before trust and rapport have been developed in the doctor-patient relationship. During my internship I was upbraided by one of my supervisors for having told a client, in the very first session, that he seemed to be too passive at work and that he tended to give up too easily. Reflections and observations of this kind, I was told, should never be made unless one is quite certain that they will be appropriately received. In brief therapy, one does not have the luxury of doing no more than applying psychic emollients so that no feathers are likely to be ruffled. A perceptive clinician can gauge how the client is reacting, and if an unfavorable response is encountered, it is usually not difficult to effect repairs. One of my safeguards is to inquire, "What do you feel about that?" whenever I make an observation. If I detect any hesitancy, a downward glance, jaw clenching, fidgeting, or any other sign suggesting that the client feels uncomfortable, I explain my benevolent intent and if necessary, apologize if I am off target.

It is interesting how a touch of benevolent manipulation can expedite matters. About 10 minutes into the initial interview with a couple, two issues emerged. (1) The 33-year-old wife was so attached to and dependent on her parents that she refused to move out of state with her husband and 4-year-old son, so that he was forced to give up a job offer. (2) The husband usually dealt with his frustrations by withdrawing and sulking. He had commented that his in-laws regarded his wife not as a 33-year-old but still saw her as 23 years of age. We discussed other issues in their troubled marriage, and I then delivered the following speech:

"This is our very first meeting. We have known each other for less than 30 minutes. According to most of the psychology books, we are supposed to spend time, perhaps several weeks, or maybe months, developing rapport and trust. At that juncture, if you have both developed faith and confidence in me, I can take the risk of sharing my candid opinions and I can make some helpful suggestions. To do so now would only annoy you and make you drop out of therapy with me. Personally, I think those prohibitions are designed not to help clients, but to keep them coming back so that the therapist can make some money. Now what should I do? Should I keep my initial impressions to myself and wait until the two of you discover that you can trust me, and that I have your best interests at heart? Or should I waste none of your time and money and tell you exactly what I think right now?"

Not surprisingly, they both said that I should be up front with them and not wait.

"Very well," I continued, "that's very brave of you. Okay, let me start with you [facing the wife]. I don't think your parents are correct in treating you like a 23-year-old, because you actually function more like a 3-year-old. In fact, the umbilical chord still needs to be cut, so you might be prenatal in some respects. [Facing the husband:] And as for you, your tendency to sulk rather than to face unpleasant issues like a man and discuss them rationally places you fair and square in the sandbox of a nursery school. Now look what I have done. I have just insulted both of you. I have disobeyed all the rules in the book by doing so. Nevertheless, I hope what I have said will be helpful and will motivate you to make some constructive changes."

The wife reacted immediately. "It is true that I am very close to my family. . . . I call my mother several times a day, but I see nothing wrong with that."

"Well," I responded, "if you think that's the norm, far be it from me to dissuade you."

The wife continued. "The job he was offered was a lateral move. If he got a job offer out of state that meant more money and a definite promotion, I would probably be willing to move there."

"Probably?" I asked.

"Okay, definitely," she answered.

"Congratulations," I said, "you have just gone from 3 to almost 33 years of age." Addressing the husband. "What do you think of that?"

"That's news to me," he said, "but I'm pleased to hear it."

"Good," said I, "but now let's see how we can transform you from a sulk into a hulk."

This leads to the issue of how to expedite the process of developing rapport and rapidly establishing a good working alliance. For example, when a 16-year-old adolescent was referred to me by the courts and commenced using a string of obscenities and invectives, I proceeded to utter a succession of expletives that turned the session into something that would have deserved one of those "X-rated: contains adult language" notices. The client was duly appreciative. "Shit, man! You're cool!" said he. Indeed, we worked very well together, and I have little doubt that my liberal use of four-letter-words served to facilitate a positive outcome.

Or take the case I reported (Lazarus, 1993) of a 39-year-old, well-dressed, attractive woman who entered my office for the first time, looked me up and down, and said "Why do you have graves outside your office?" I was completely baffled. "I have graves outside my office?" said I, imitating Carl Rogers. "Look out the window, dummy!" she replied. Most clients are unlikely to assail therapists in this manner. When responding to any behavior, therapists have milliseconds to decide what to say or do. In this case, one could remain silent; one could say, "Do you always come on this strong?"—the possible response-couplets are exceedingly diverse. Imagine a noxious therapist who becomes defensive and says, "I don't like being spoken to in this way!" When training my students, I like listening to tape recordings of sessions and switching off the tape at various points to discuss the range of response-couplets that might be neutral, positive, or negative.

My response to the command "Look out the window, dummy!" was to peer out of my office window. Two new flower beds had been installed in the grass alongside the front walk. It was early spring, and the shoots had yet to emerge from the soil. "Well, since you ask," I said, "I have just buried one of my clinical failures in the one grave, and the other is earmarked for you if you turn out to be an uncooperative client." The twinkle in her eye told me that my response was an appropriate one. Some additional banter followed, and the client then discussed the profound concerns for which she was seeking help. Had I responded not ironically but in a stodgy or serious way—"Oh, those are merely newly planted flower beds"—I doubt whether the necessary rapport would have developed, because the client strongly favored "people with a sense of humor." Indeed, each session would commence with some friendly banter and jesting, followed by attention to the serious issues for which she sought psychotherapy.

Humor—including jokes, amusing parables, and whimsical anecdotes—has a definite place in psychotherapy. Kwee (1996) wrote: "Remarkably, when following up clients after many years, they tended to remember a relevant joke I had told them and continued to draw comfort from a 'wise narrative' I had related." His article "Travelling in the Footsteps of Hotei towards the 21st Century" (Kwee & Holdstock, 1996) discusses how therapists can expedite therapy with certain clients by invoking "the psychology of happiness, humor, joy, laughing and smiling . . . [versus] academic seriousness" (p. 175).

Let me mention one more common time waster. There is a far-reaching myth that if ideas, strategies, solutions and, decisions do not come from the clients themselves but are prompted by the therapist, their worth, value, and benefit are seriously diluted. Consequently, many clinicians wait for clients to see the light, draw conclusions, gain insights, and come to their own realizations. In many instances, these therapists could very well wait forever! When time is of the essence, waiting around for self-discovery makes no sense at all. I will inform, prompt, and if necessary urge the client to consider a course of action; I will make observations, share impressions, offer advice, and state opinions. If the client is not ready to hear them or act on them, no harm is done (despite the tomes that have been written about the presumed dangers of "premature interpretations"). In these cases, in my experience, clients simply do not comply with the recommendations or suggestions. However, initial refutations and denials are followed by a newfound ownership—as if the client had indeed reached the same conclusions independently.

Here is a typical sequence:

THERAPIST: Your mother probably thinks that you want to quit school, and that is presumably why she wants your Uncle Billy to persuade your dad to pay the fees for the graduate course. I'll bet that next week when Billy is in town, he will discuss this matter with your father.

CLIENT: I don't think so. But if my mom did ask him, it is likely that Billy would want to lean on my dad for his own reasons.

THERAPIST: And what would those reasons be?

CLIENT: I can't say for sure, but it is probably Billy's way of letting my dad know that he is cheap and that Billy put his three kids through college and then picked up the tab for their postgraduate work—kind of lording it over him.

THERAPIST: So your mother hasn't got wind of the fact that you spoke to Charles [his older brother] about dropping out of school, and when she hinted to your father about paying the tuition, he didn't play dumb?

CLIENT: I don't think Charles would have said anything.

At this point, the matter was dropped. Everyone knows that arguing with clients is usually inadvisable. But "right-brain seeds" had been planted. The point that the therapist was trying to convey had to do with the family dynamics. These people were almost always indirect and acted like cerebral detectives, second-guessing everyone's putative plans and motives, and manipulating each other into talking on the other person's behalf. Previously, the client had been asked why he didn't simply approach his father for the money instead of waiting for his mother or someone else to do so for him. "Because it would be useless to do so, and I don't want to engage in exercises of futility," said he.

Two days later the client called and said: "I want to run something by you. It occurred to me that Charles probably blabbed to everyone that I was thinking about quitting school and that this really upset my mom. She knew it all depended on whether or not the tuition would get paid. So she must have figured out that Billy would be the right one to chat to my dad—after all, everyone knows how generous he's been with his kids. But why the heck should I hide behind my mother's apron strings and get Billy to do the talking for me? So what do you think of my taking the bull by the horns and asking my dad for the money?"

Touchdown!

Epilogue

T he view of a two-way street between laboratory and clinic has characterized my thinking for many years. "The process of discovery that is carried on within the clinical practices of some therapists is the equivalent of research, [and] . . . ideas formulated in the clinic, provided that they are amenable to verification or disproof, can send scientists scurrying off into laboratories to subject the claims of efficacy to controlled tests" (Lazarus & Davison, 1971, pp. 196–197). Moreover, "innovations by clinicians are the lifeblood of advances in the development of new therapeutic interventions" (Davison & Lazarus, 1994, p. 157). I adhere to this perspective even more strongly today. The notions and strategies described in this book are based largely on outcome and follow-up inquiries that I have conducted over a span of some three dozen post-doctoral years of clinical practice.

Perhaps *follow-ups* have been the single most important course of action from which I have derived my assumptions and inferences about the enterprise of therapy. During the 1960s, which was the heyday of my behavioristic zeal, my follow-ups showed that many treatment gains were short-lived. The dreaded "symptom substitution" was rarely a factor, but after receiving the usual range of "behavior therapy" techniques, clients tended to relapse more often than my colleagues seemed to admit. Careful scrutiny of those cases who failed to maintain their gains persuaded me that they had learned an insufficiently wide range of coping responses. Thus, I advocated "broad-spectrum behavior therapy" in place of the more circumscribed methods that were in vogue. This evolved into the seven-pronged multimodal approach.

The multimodal approach has always been relatively brief, but in the present era of managed health care, the need for even greater brevity has become a necessity. Is it possible to remain focused, to accelerate the speed or pace of treatment, without sacrificing too much detail? It is my hope that readers of this book will discover a modus operandi for achieving this double-barreled goal.

To recapitulate, some of the main points of view and tactics espoused throughout this book are:

1. The significance and expedience of the BASIC I.D. and its derivative procedures (Second-Order Assessments, Bridging, Tracking, Modality Profiles, and Structural Profiles)
2. The need for a set of flexible, humanistic, and broad-based but empirically verifiable assessment and treatment procedures
3. The importance of combining appropriate relationship styles with empirically validated treatments of choice
4. Avoiding some common traps and myths that undermine the process of effective therapy
5. The willingness and capacity to transcend certain boundaries to facilitate salubrious outcomes
6. The importance of eschewing theories that are not amenable to verification or disproof
7. The dangers and pitfalls of theoretical integration and the virtues of technical eclecticism
8. The overall advantages of an active rather than a passive or purely reflective therapeutic stance
9. Pragmatic insights and experientially focused exercises from fairly detailed accounts of MMT for problems frequently encountered in clinical practice — inhibited sexual desire, dysthymia, and dysfunctional couples
10. Avoiding some common time wasters

Nevertheless, diligent readers who have carefully perused this entire book will undoubtedly encounter certain clients who remain unresponsive to their interventions. In that case, what does one do? To whom does one turn? Peer consultation is the obvious solution, and in this day and age there are several productive avenues to pursue.

When I get stuck, bogged down, or bewildered or feel out of my depth, I have recourse to several resources.

1. I am part of an ongoing supervision group that meets once a month. There are four of us who spend approximately 2 to 3 hours discussing our difficult clients. We offer one another recommendations and suggestions for resolving impasses.
2. Close collaboration since 1972 with Allen Fay, M.D., an extremely creative Manhattan-based psychiatrist, has been a source of inspiration and education.
3. My son, Clifford N. Lazarus, Ph.D., has areas of expertise that lie out side my own domain, and we consult each other about problematic situations and sometimes see clients together.
4. Many of my colleagues at Rutgers University have kindly offered wise counsel and intellectual stimulation over the years.

Frankly, I have usually found these resources far more useful than attending workshops, postgraduate seminars, and other formal training avenues. Thus, I strongly advise everyone to establish a similar network of professional connections. But what of the therapist who practices in a rural area in which his or her nearest professional colleague is perhaps hundreds of miles away? Thanks to modern technology, access to the Internet can serve a most useful function. In addition to bulletin boards and other resources on the World Wide Web, there are numerous psychotherapy lists one may join. From time to time, when I have posed clinical conundrums on the Internet, I was amazed at the number of helpful hints I received, often from total strangers. My favorite list is the SSCPNET (Society for a Science of Clinical Psychology), managed by a branch of Division 12 of the American Psychological Association. As long as one does not abuse the privilege and opportunity, this is a marvelous way to obtain input from some of the very best thinkers in the field. The SSCPNET also has a page on the World Wide Web.

It is noteworthy that most American psychologists feel a need for advanced training seminars, certificate programs, and hands-on instruction. However, psychologists in Europe, after simply reading about the multimodal orientation, proceeded to practice MMT and even launched multimodal training centers. I visited the Netherlands, where, under the auspices of Dr. M. G. T. Kwee, several therapists have applied MMT. It was gratifying to note how expertly they utilized the methods. Indeed, in some respects they had enhanced and augmented the fundamental approach. Similarly, a visit with Stephen Palmer, who has developed a series of training modules as the Director of the Centre for Multimodal Therapy in London, revealed his clinical and conceptual expertise. Professor W. Dryden of Goldsmith's College (affiliated with the University of London, England) is also involved at the Centre. In Argentina, Dr. Roberto Kertész and several of his colleagues have put MMT to good use, offered training seminars, and translated several of my books into Spanish.

Whereas many professionals remain impressed by books and concepts that are complex and indeterminate, if not incomprehensible, my view is that any clinical approach that is not easy to understand, easy to remember, and easy to apply is unworthy of serious attention. I trust that the reader will agree that the notions espoused throughout this book fall into the latter rather than the former category.

Multimodal Life History Inventory

The purpose of this inventory is to obtain a comprehensive picture of your background. In psychotherapy records are necessary since they permit a more thorough dealing with one's problems. By completing these questions as fully and as accurately as you can, you will facilitate your therapeutic program. You are requested to answer these routine questions in your own time instead of using up your actual consulting time (please feel free to use extra sheets if you need additional answer space).

It is understandable that you might be concerned about what happens to the information about you because much or all of this information is highly personal. Case records are strictly confidential.

Second edition, 1991
First edition, 1980, published as the Multimodal Life History Questionnaire

Research Press
2612 North Mattis Avenue
Champaign, Illinois 61821

GENERAL INFORMATION

Date: _____

Name: _____

Address: _____

Telephone numbers: Day_____ Evening_____

Age: _____ Occupation: _____ Sex: ___ M ___ F

Date of birth: _____ Place of birth: _____ Religion: _____

Height: _____ Weight: _____ Does your weight fluctuate? ___ Yes ___ No If yes, by how much? _____

Do you have a family physician? ___Yes ___ No

Name of family physician: _____ Telephone number: _____

By whom were you referred? _____

Marital status (check one): ___ Single ___ Engaged ___ Married ___ Separated ___ Divorced

___ Widowed ___ Living with someone ___ Remarried: How many times? _____

Do you live in: ___ House ___ Room ___ Apartment ___ Other: _____

With whom do you live? (check all that apply): ___ Self ___ Parents ___ Spouse ___ Roommate

___ Child(ren) ___ Friend(s) ___ Others (specify): _____

What sort of work are you doing now? _____

Does your present work satisfy you? ___ Yes ___ No

If no, please explain: _____

_____

What kind of jobs have you held in the past? _____

_____

Have you been in therapy before or received any professional assistance for your problems? ___ Yes ___ No

Have you ever been hospitalized for psychological/psychiatric problems? ___ Yes ___ No

If yes, when and where? _____

_____

Have you ever attempted suicide? ___ Yes ___ No

Does any member of your family suffer from an "emotional" or "mental disorder"? ___ Yes ___ No

Has any relative attempted or committed suicide? ___ Yes ___ No

PERSONAL AND SOCIAL HISTORY

Father: Name: _____ Age: _____

Occupation: _____ Health: _____

If deceased, give his age at time of death: _____ How old were you at the time? _____

Cause of death: _____

Mother: Name: _____ Age: _____

Occupation: _____ Health: _____

If deceased, give her age at time of death: _____ How old were you at the time? _____

Cause of death: _____

Siblings: Age(s) of brother(s): _____ Age(s) of sister(s): _____

Any significant details about siblings: _____

_____

_____

If you were not brought up by your parents, who raised you and between what years?

_____

_____

Give a description of your father's (or father substitute's) personality and his attitude toward you (past and present):

_____

_____

_____

_____

_____

Give a description of your mother's (or mother substitute's) personality and her attitude toward you (past and present):

_____

_____

_____

_____

_____

In what ways were you disciplined or punished by your parents?

_____

_____

_____

_____

Give an impression of your home atmosphere (i.e., the home in which you grew up). Mention state of compatibility between parents and between children.

_____

_____

_____

_____

_____

_____

Were you able to confide in your parents? ____ Yes ____ No

Basically, did you feel loved and respected by your parents? ____ Yes ____ No

If you have a stepparent, give your age when your parent remarried: _____

Has anyone (parents, relatives, friends) ever interfered in your marriage, occupation, etc.? ____ Yes ____ No

If yes, please describe briefly: _____

_____

_____

Scholastic strengths: _____

Scholastic weaknesses: _____

What was the last grade completed (or highest degree)? _____

Check any of the following that applied during your childhood/adolescence:

____ Happy childhood	____ Not enough friends	____ Sexually abused
____ Unhappy childhood	____ School problems	____ Severely bullied or teased
____ Emotional/behavior problems	____ Financial problems	____ Eating disorder
____ Legal trouble	____ Strong religious convictions	____ Others: _____
____ Death in family	____ Drug use	_____
____ Medical problems	____ Used alcohol	_____
____ Ignored	____ Severely punished	_____

DESCRIPTION OF PRESENTING PROBLEMS

State in your own words the nature of your main problems: _____
_____
_____
_____
_____
_____

On the scale below, please estimate the severity of your problem(s):

____ Mildly upsetting   ____ Moderately upsetting   ____ Very severe   ____ Extremely severe   ____ Totally incapacitating

When did your problems begin? _____
_____

What seems to worsen your problems? _____
_____

What have you tried that has been helpful? _____
_____

How satisfied are you with your life as a whole these days?

        Not at all satisfied   1   2   3   4   5   6   7   Very satisfied

How would you rate your overall level of tension during the past month?

        Relaxed   1   2   3   4   5   6   7   Tense

EXPECTATIONS REGARDING THERAPY

In a few words, what do you think therapy is all about? _____
_____
_____

How long do you think your therapy should last? _____
_____
_____

What personal qualities do you think the ideal therapist should possess? _____
_____
_____

MODALITY ANALYSIS OF CURRENT PROBLEMS

The following section is designed to help you describe your current problems in greater detail and to identify problems that might otherwise go unnoticed. This will enable us to design a comprehensive treatment program and tailor it to your specific needs. The following section is organized according to the seven modalities of Behaviors, Feelings, Physical Sensations, Images, Thoughts, Interpersonal Relationships, and Biological Factors.

BEHAVIORS

Check any of the following behaviors that often apply to you:

___ Overeat	___ Loss of control	___ Phobic avoidance	___ Crying
___ Take drugs	___ Suicidal attempts	___ Spend too much money	___ Outbursts of temper
___ Unassertive	___ Compulsions	___ Can't keep a job	___ Others: _____
___ Odd behavior	___ Smoke	___ Insomnia	_____
___ Drink too much	___ Withdrawal	___ Take too many risks	_____
___ Work too hard	___ Nervous tics	___ Lazy	
___ Procrastination	___ Concentration difficulties	___ Eating problems	
___ Impulsive reactions	___ Sleep disturbance	___ Aggressive behavior	

What are some special talents or skills that you feel proud of? _____

_____

What would you like to start doing? _____

_____

What would you like to stop doing? _____

_____

How is your free time spent? _____

_____

What kind of hobbies or leisure activities do you enjoy or find relaxing? _____

_____

Do you have trouble relaxing or enjoying weekends and vacations?   ___ Yes   ___ No

If yes, please explain: _____

_____

_____

If you could have any two wishes, what would they be? _____

_____

_____

FEELINGS

Check any of the following feelings that often apply to you:

___ Angry	___ Fearful	___ Happy	___ Hopeful	___ Bored	___ Optimistic
___ Annoyed	___ Panicky	___ Conflicted	___ Helpless	___ Restless	___ Tense
___ Sad	___ Energetic	___ Shameful	___ Relaxed	___ Lonely	___ Others: _____
___ Depressed	___ Envious	___ Regretful	___ Jealous	___ Contented	_____
___ Anxious	___ Guilty	___ Hopeless	___ Unhappy	___ Excited	_____

List your five main fears:

1. _____

2. _____

3. _____

4. _____

5. _____

What are some positive feelings you have experienced recently?_____

_____

_____

When are you most likely to lose control of your feelings? _____

_____

_____

Describe any situations that make you feel calm or relaxed: _____

_____

_____

PHYSICAL SENSATIONS

Check any of the following physical sensations that often apply to you:

___ Abdominal pain	___ Bowel disturbances	___ Hear things	___ Blackouts
___ Pain or burning with urination	___ Tingling	___ Watery eyes	___ Excessive sweating
___ Menstrual difficulties	___ Numbness	___ Flushes	___ Visual disturbances
___ Headaches	___ Stomach trouble	___ Nausea	___ Hearing problems
___ Dizziness	___ Tics	___ Skin problems	___ Others: _____
___ Palpitations	___ Fatigue	___ Dry mouth	_____
___ Muscle spasms	___ Twitches	___ Burning or itching skin	_____
___ Tension	___ Back pain	___ Chest pains	
___ Sexual disturbances	___ Tremors	___ Rapid heart beat	
___ Unable to relax	___ Fainting spells	___ Don't like to be touched	

What sensations are:

Pleasant for you? _____

Unpleasant for you? _____

IMAGES

Check any of the following that apply to you:

I picture myself:

___ Being happy	___ Being talked about	___ Being trapped
___ Being hurt	___ Being aggressive	___ Being laughed at
___ Not coping	___ Being helpless	___ Being promiscuous
___ Succeeding	___ Hurting others	___ Others: _____
___ Losing control	___ Being in charge	_____
___ Being followed	___ Failing	_____

I have:

___ Pleasant sexual images	___ Seduction images
___ Unpleasant childhood images	___ Images of being loved
___ Negative body image	___ Others: _____
___ Unpleasant sexual images	_____
___ Lonely images	_____

Describe a very pleasant image, mental picture, or fantasy: _____

_____

_____

Describe a very unpleasant image, mental picture, or fantasy: _____

_____

_____

Describe your image of a completely "safe place": _____

_____

_____

Describe any persistent or disturbing images that interfere with your daily functioning: _____

_____

_____

How often do you have nightmares? _____

THOUGHTS

Check each of the following that you might use to describe yourself:

____ Intelligent	____ A nobody	____ Inadequate	____ Concentration difficulties	____ Lazy
____ Confident	____ Useless	____ Confused	____ Memory problems	____ Untrustworthy
____ Worthwhile	____ Evil	____ Ugly	____ Attractive	____ Dishonest
____ Ambitious	____ Crazy	____ Stupid	____ Can't make decisions	____ Others: ____
____ Sensitive	____ Morally degenerate	____ Naive	____ Suicidal ideas	_____
____ Loyal	____ Considerate	____ Honest	____ Persevering	_____
____ Trustworthy	____ Deviant	____ Incompetent	____ Good sense of humor	
____ Full of regrets	____ Unattractive	____ Horrible thoughts	____ Hard working	
____ Worthless	____ Unlovable	____ Conflicted	____ Undesirable	

What do you consider to be your craziest thought or idea? _____

_____

Are you bothered by thoughts that occur over and over again? ____Yes ____ No

If yes, what are these thoughts?_____

_____

What worries do you have that may negatively affect your mood or behavior? _____

_____

On each of the following items, please circle the number that most accurately reflects your opinions:

	Strongly disagree	Disagree	Neutral	Agree	Strongly agree
I should not make mistakes.	1	2	3	4	5
I should be good at everything I do.	1	2	3	4	5
When I do not know something, I should pretend that I do.	1	2	3	4	5
I should not disclose personal information.	1	2	3	4	5
I am a victim of circumstances.	1	2	3	4	5
My life is controlled by outside forces.	1	2	3	4	5
Other people are happier than I am.	1	2	3	4	5
It is very important to please other people.	1	2	3	4	5
Play it safe; don't take any risks.	1	2	3	4	5
I don't deserve to be happy.	1	2	3	4	5
If I ignore my problems, they will disappear.	1	2	3	4	5
It is my responsibility to make other people happy.	1	2	3	4	5
I should strive for perfection.	1	2	3	4	5
Basically, there are two ways of doing things—the right way and the wrong way.	1	2	3	4	5
I should never be upset.	1	2	3	4	5

INTERPERSONAL RELATIONSHIPS

Friendships

Do you make friends easily? ____Yes ____ No   Do you keep them? ____ Yes ____ No

Did you date much during high school? ____Yes ____ No   College? ____ Yes ____ No

Were you ever bullied or severely teased? ____Yes ____ No

Describe any relationship that gives you:

Joy: _____

_____

Grief: _____

_____

Rate the degree to which you generally feel relaxed and comfortable in social situations:

            Very relaxed   1   2   3   4   5   6   7   Very anxious

Do you have one or more friends with whom you feel comfortable sharing your most private thoughts? ____Yes ____ No

Marriage (or a committed relationship)

How long did you know your spouse before your engagement? _____

How long were you engaged before you got married? _____

How long have you been married? _____

What is your spouse's age? _____ His/her occupation? _____

Describe your spouse's personality: _____

_____

_____

What do you like most about your spouse? _____

_____

_____

What do you like least about your spouse? _____

_____

_____

What factors detract from your marital satisfaction? _____

_____

_____

On the scale below, please indicate how satisfied you are with your marriage:

           Very dissatisfied   1   2   3   4   5   6   7   Very satisfied

How do you get along with your partner's friends and family?

           Very poorly   1   2   3   4   5   6   7   Very well

How many children do you have? _____

Please give their names and ages: _____

_____

_____

Do any of your children present special problems? ____Yes ____ No

If yes, please describe: _____

_____

Any significant details about a previous marriage(s)?_____

_____

_____

Sexual Relationships

Describe your parents' attitude toward sex. Was sex discussed in your home? _____

_____

When and how did you derive your first knowledge of sex?_____

_____

_____

When did you first become aware of your own sexual impulses? _____

_____

_____

Have you ever experienced any anxiety or guilt arising out of sex or masturbation? ____Yes ____ No

If yes, please explain: _____

_____

Any relevant details regarding your first or subsequent sexual experiences? _____

_____

_____

Is your present sex life satisfactory? ____Yes ____ No

If no, please explain: _____

_____

_____

Provide information about any significant homosexual reactions or relationships: _____

_____

_____

Please note any sexual concerns not discussed above: _____

_____

_____

Other Relationships

Are there any problems in your relationships with people at work? ____Yes ____ No

If yes, please describe: _____

_____

Please complete the following:

One of the ways people hurt me is: _____

_____

I could shock you by: _____

_____

My spouse (or boyfriend/girlfriend) would describe me as: _____

_____

My best friend thinks I am: _____

_____

People who dislike me: _____

_____

Are you currently troubled by any past rejections or loss of a love relationship? ____Yes ____ No

If yes, please explain: _____

_____

_____

BIOLOGICAL FACTORS

Do you have any current concerns about your physical health?   ____Yes   ____ No

If yes, please specify: _____

_____

_____

_____

Please list any medications you are currently taking: _____

_____

_____

Do you eat three well-balanced meals each day?   ____Yes   ____ No

Do you get regular physical exercise?   ____ Yes   ____ No

If yes, what type and how often? _____

_____

_____

Please list any significant medical problems that apply to you or to members of your family: _____

_____

_____

_____

Please describe any surgery you have had (give dates): _____

_____

_____

_____

Please describe any physical handicap(s) you have: _____

_____

_____

Menstrual History

Age at first period: _____ Were you informed? ____ Yes ____ No   Did it come as a shock? ____Yes ____ No

Are you regular? ____Yes ____ No   Duration: _____   Do you have pain? ____ Yes ____ No

Do your periods affect your moods? ____Yes ____ No   Date of last period: _____

Check any of the following that apply to you:

	Never	Rarely	Occasionally	Frequently	Daily
Muscle weakness					
Tranquilizers					
Diuretics					
Diet pills					
Marijuana					
Hormones					
Sleeping pills					
Aspirin					
Cocaine					
Pain killers					
Narcotics					
Stimulants					
Hallucinogens (e.g., LSD)					
Laxatives					
Cigarettes					
Tobacco (specify)					
Coffee					
Alcohol					
Birth control pills					
Vitamins					
Undereat					
Overeat					
Eat junk foods					
Diarrhea					
Constipation					
Gas					
Indigestion					
Nausea					
Vomiting					
Heartburn					
Dizziness					
Palpitations					
Fatigue					
Allergies					
High blood pressure					
Chest pain					
Shortness of breath					
Insomnia					
Sleep too much					
Fitful sleep					
Early morning awakening					
Earaches					
Headaches					
Backaches					
Bruise or bleed easily					
Weight problems					
Others:					

STRUCTURAL PROFILE

Directions: Rate yourself on the following dimensions on a seven-point scale with "1" being the lowest and "7" being the highest.

BEHAVIORS:	Some people may be described as "doers"—they are action oriented, they like to busy themselves, get things done, take on various projects. How much of a doer are you?	1	2	3	4	5	6	7
FEELINGS:	Some people are very emotional and may or may not express it. How emotional are you? How deeply do you feel things? How passionate are you?	1	2	3	4	5	6	7
PHYSICAL SENSATIONS:	Some people attach a lot of value to sensory experiences, such as sex, food, music, art, and other "sensory delights." Others are very much aware of minor aches, pains, and discomforts. How "tuned into" your sensations are you?	1	2	3	4	5	6	7
MENTAL IMAGES:	How much fantasy or daydreaming do you engage in? This is separate from thinking or planning. This is "thinking in pictures," visualizing real or imagined experiences, letting your mind roam. How much are you into imagery?	1	2	3	4	5	6	7
THOUGHTS:	Some people are very analytical and like to plan things. They like to reason things through. How much of a "thinker" and "planner" are you?	1	2	3	4	5	6	7
INTERPERSONAL RELATIONSHIPS:	How important are other people to you? This is your self-rating as a social being. How important are close friendships to you, the tendency to gravitate toward people, the desire for intimacy? The opposite of this is being a "loner."	1	2	3	4	5	6	7
BIOLOGICAL FACTORS:	Are you healthy and health conscious? Do you avoid bad habits like smoking, too much alcohol, drinking a lot of coffee, overeating, etc.? Do you exercise regularly, get enough sleep, avoid junk foods, and generally take care of your body?	1	2	3	4	5	6	7

Please describe any significant childhood (or other) memories and experiences you think your therapist should be aware of:

_____

_____

_____

_____

_____

_____

_____

_____

_____

_____

_____

_____

_____

_____

_____

_____

_____

_____

_____

_____

_____

_____

_____

_____

_____

_____

_____

Structural Profile Inventory

IN THE SPACE NEXT TO EACH OF THE FOLLOWING ITEMS, PLEASE WRITE DOWN THE NUMBER THAT MOST ACCURATELY REFLECTS YOUR OPINION:

Strongly disagree 1	Moderately disagree 2	Slightly disagree 3	Neutral 4	Slightly agree 5	Moderately agree 6	Strongly agree 7

NAME _____   DATE _____

1. _____ I tend to plan things and think about them a great deal.
2. _____ I often imagine situations "in pictures."
3. _____ In making a decision, I often let my feelings and emotions determine what I should do.
4. _____ Basically, I'm in excellent health.
5. _____ I can form clear mental pictures.
6. _____ I get sufficient rest and relaxation.
7. _____ I would probably be described as "active and energetic."
8. _____ I would *not* be described as a "loner."
9. _____ I am a very active person.
10. _____ I am a "people person."
11. _____ I follow good nutritional habits.
12. _____ Most of the time, I'd rather be with other people than alone.
13. _____ I often engage in intellectual (cognitive) activities.
14. _____ I can form vivid pictures in my imagination.
15. _____ I avoid overeating, too much alcohol, and keep away from harmful things such as drugs and tobacco.

143

16. _____ I am tuned in to my senses—what I see, hear, taste, smell, and touch.
17. _____ Friendships are very important to me.
18. _____ I consider myself sensual and sexual.
19. _____ I usually think before acting.
20. _____ I am aware of the ways in which my senses react to different stimuli.
21. _____ I am an imaginative person.
22. _____ I have very deep feelings and notions.
23. _____ I reason most things out quite thoroughly.
24. _____ I keep busy doing things.
25. _____ I think more in pictures than in words.
26. _____ I take good care of my body.
27. _____ I keep occupied and on the go.
28. _____ I pay a lot of attention to my feelings and emotions.
29. _____ I have several close or intimate friendships.
30. _____ I focus a great deal on my bodily sensations.
31. _____ I am a very emotional person.
32. _____ I analyze things quite thoroughly.
33. _____ My feelings are easily aroused and/or changeable.
34. _____ I am full of pep and vigor.
35. _____ Most of my five senses are very keen (smelling, tasting, seeing, hearing, touching).

SPI Scoring Key

- *Behavior:*   7, 9, 24, 27, 34
- *Affect:*   3, 22, 28, 31, 33
- *Sensation:*   16, 18, 20, 30, 35
- *Imagery:*   2, 5, 14, 21, 25
- *Cognition:*   1, 13, 19, 23, 32
- *Interpersonal:*   8, 10, 12, 17, 29
- *Drugs/Health:*   4, 6, 11, 15, 26

Expanded Structural Profile

NAME _____ DATE _____

SEVEN DIMENSIONS OF PERSONALITY

1. Doing . . . Action =	BEHAVIOR	B
2. Feelings . . . Mood Emotions =	AFFECT	A
3. Sensing . . . (sight, sound, touch, etc.) =	SENSATION	S
4. Imagining . . . Fantasy . . . Visualizing =	IMAGERY	I
5. Thinking . . . Interpreting . . . "Self-Talk" =	COGNITION	C
6. Social . . . Relating =	INTERPERSONAL	I.
7. Biological . . . Physical . . . Health =	DRUGS	D.

1: BEHAVIOR

"Behaviors" are our actions, reactions, and conduct. Behavior is how we *act* in various situations or under certain conditions. Examples of behaviors include: sleeping, eating, playing tennis, crying, walking, yelling, watching television, reading, riding a bicycle, etc. Thus, just about anything we do can be considered a behavior.

Some people may be described as "doers"—they are action-oriented; they like to keep busy, get things done, take on various projects. On the scale below, circle the number that best reflects to what degree you are a doer.

Very little			Moderately			Very much	
1	2	3	4	5	6	7

In the space below, try to make a note of at least one specific behavior that you would like to do *less* of, and also one specific behavior you would like to do *more* of.

- I would like to do less (or stop):
- I would like to do more (or start):

2: AFFECT

"Affect" is the psychological term for *feelings, moods, and emotions*. Some affects are positive (such as joy), while others can be characterized as negative (such as depression). Other examples of affects include: happiness, annoyance, contentment, anxiety, jealousy, anger, excitement, guilt, and shame.

Some people are very emotional but may or may not openly express emotions. How emotional are you? How deeply do you feel things? How passionate are you?

Very little			Moderately		Very much	
1	2	3	4	5	6	7

In the space below, try to make a note of at least one emotion you would like to feel less of and at least one emotion you would like to experience more often.

- I would like to feel less:
- I would like to experience more:

3: SENSATION

"Sensation" refers to the five basic human senses: *sight, sound, smell, touch, and taste*. In addition, the sensation dimension involves elements of sensuality and sexuality. Sometimes sensory experience is pleasant (for example, sexual intimacy, the smell of a fresh rose, or the taste of apple pie) while at other times sensations can be unpleasant (for example, the pain of a stiff neck or a tension headache, or the smell of rotten eggs).

Some people attach a lot of value to sensory experiences, such as sex, art, food, music, and other "sensory pleasures." Some people often focus on their sensations and pay much attention to pleasant and unpleasant inner experiences (such as inner calm and relaxation, or minor aches, pains, and discomfort). How "tuned in" to your sensations are you?

Very little			Moderately		Very much	
1	2	3	4	5	6	7

Below, make a note of some sensations you would like to experience less of and more of.

- I would like to experience less:
- I would like to experience more:

4: IMAGERY

"Imagery" refers to people's ability to form *mental pictures* or representations of actual or imagined things, events, and situations. When we fantasize, daydream, or just see pictures in our "mind's eye," we are engaging in mental imagery.

How much fantasy or daydreaming do you engage in? How much and how clearly do you "think in pictures" or see things projected onto the screen of your imagination? (This is separate from thinking or planning.) How much are you into imagery?

Very little			**Moderately**			**Very much**
1	2	3	4	5	6	7

Make a note below of at least one thing, event, or, situation you would like to imagine less of and at least one thing you would like to imagine more.

- I would like to imagine less:
- I would like to imagine more:

5. COGNITION

"Cognition" is *thinking*, or the mental faculty or process by which information is obtained. Reasoning, knowledge, and thought are all aspects of cognition. Often, people's thinking takes the form of private "self-talk." Self-talk is the tendency we all have to silently talk to ourselves and to tell ourselves things in the privacy of our own thoughts. Sometimes, our self-talk or cognitions make us feel good about ourselves. For example, when we tell ourselves things like "That was a really good job I did" or "I'm really an okay person," we tend to feel good. At other times, however, our cognitions can make us feel unhappy with ourselves. For instance, when tell ourselves things like "I'll never be able to get the hang of this" or "I must really be a worthless person," we tend to react with unpleasant feelings.

Some people may be described as "thinkers" or "planners"—they are very analytical and reflective and tend to think things through. How much do you "talk to yourself?" To what extent are you a thinker or a planner?

Very little			**Moderately**			**Very much**
1	2	3	4	5	6	7

Below, try to make a note of some cognitions you would like to have less often and some thoughts you would like to have more often.

- I would like to think less:
- I would like to think more:

6. INTERPERSONAL RELATIONSHIPS

Most of us live in richly social environments in which we are constantly interacting with other people across a variety of situations. Not surprisingly, some of our personal interactions are pleasant (for example, making love or playing a friendly game of cards) while others are not so pleasant (for example, fighting and arguing).

This is your self-rating as a social being. How important are other people to you? How important are close friendships to you? How important is the desire for intimacy, the tendency to gravitate toward people? The opposite of this is being a "loner." To what extent are you a "people person"?

Very little			**Moderately**		**Very much**	
1	2	3	4	5	6	7

Below, try to note some interpersonal or social activities you would like to decrease and others you would like to increase.

- I would like to decrease:
- I would like to increase:

7. DRUGS/BIOLOGICAL/HEALTH FACTORS

When you come right down to it, we are basically biological, biochemical creatures governed by the activities of our body and brain chemistry. Many of the things we do (that is, many of our behaviors) impact on our biology and hence influence how we think, act, and feel. Included in this aspect of human personality are such things as our general eating and exercise habits, how much alcohol we drink, whether or not we smoke or take drugs, whether or not we should lose some weight or get more regular sleep, etc.

Are you healthy and health-concious? Do you avoid bad habits like smoking, too much alcohol or caffeine, overeating, etc.? Do you exercise regularly, get enough sleep, limit junk food, and generally take care of your body?

Very little			**Moderately**		**Very much**	
1	2	3	4	5	6	7

Below, note some things concerning biological factors that you would like to decrease and some things relating to biology you would like to increase?

- I would like to decrease:
- I would like to increase:

COMMENTS OR ADDITIONAL INFORMATION

[Space is allowed here for anything the client wants to add.]

Marital Satisfaction Questionnaire
(Revised)

NAME: _____ DATE: _____

DIRECTIONS

1	2	3	4	5	6	7	8	9	10
Not pleased			**Somewhat pleased**				**Very pleased**		

In the first space after each item please write down the number that most closely and honestly reflects your present feelings about your marriage/relationship or spouse/partner. In the second space, estimate how you believe your spouse/partner would respond to the item if he/she were completing the questionnaire. Work as quickly as possible, trying not to spend too much time on any one item.

I AM:

1. Pleased with the amount we talk to each other. _____ _____
2. Pleased with the *quality* of our communication (e.g., pleasant, constructive, vs. insensitive, hostile, etc.). _____ _____
3. Satisfied with our sex life. _____ _____
4. Satisfied with the way we are spending/managing money. _____ _____
5. Satisfied with the amount of time we spend together. _____ _____

6. Happy with our social life and friends we share in common. _____ _____

7. Pleased with the kind of parent my spouse/partner is. (If you have no children, rate your level of satisfaction about this fact.) _____ _____

8. Of the opinion that my spouse/partner is "on my team." _____ _____

9. Pleased with our leisure time together (e.g., vacations, sports, outings, etc.). _____ _____

10. Basically in agreement with my spouse's/partner's outlook on life (e.g., values, religious beliefs, political ideas, etc.) _____ _____

11. Content with degree of affection that is given and received. _____ _____

12. Able to trust what my spouse/partner says and does. _____ _____

13. Content about my partner's smoking, drinking, or other habits. _____ _____

14. Pleased with my relationship(s) with members of my spouse's/partner's family (e.g., his or her parents, siblings, and other relatives). _____ _____

15. Pleased with the way my spouse/partner relates to members of my own family (i.e., your parents, siblings, etc.). _____ _____

16. Pleased with my spouse's overall appearance. _____ _____

INTERPRETATION

Overall totals are less relevant than scores on individual items. Since scores range between 16 and 160, a tally of under 80 would signify significant marital dissatisfaction. Nevertheless, it is most productive to discuss individual scores, inquiring exactly why a particular item merited a 9 or 10, whereas another only justified a 3 or 4. Examining specific discrepancies in partners' estimations of the other person's ratings also proves productive.

1995 Article

Different Types of Eclecticism and Integration: Let's Be Aware of the Dangers[1]

Arnold A. Lazarus[2,3]

An eclectic stance is warranted only when well-documented treatments of choice do not exist for a particular disorder, or when these established methods are not achieving the desired results. But great care must be exercised when scouring the field for potentially effective methods that have yet to be scientifically tested. It is all too easy to confuse observations with theories and to obfuscate matters by endorsing superfluous notions. To apply certain procedures that psychodynamic clinicians employ, or to capitalize on techniques typically utilized by gestalt therapists, does not translate into "doing psychodynamic therapy" or endorsing gestalt therapy per se. There does not appear to be a single instance wherein a blend of different theories produced a more powerful technique, but there are numerous cases where techniques drawn from different disciplines have enriched clinicians' armamentaria. A brief account of an agoraphobic woman who received eclectic therapy helps underscore the pros, cons, and dangers of eclecticism and integration.

KEY WORDS: treatments of choice; theoretical consistency; behavioral interpretations; agoraphobia; psychodynamics vs applied psychology; active ingredients.

INTRODUCTION

A man enters a bar, orders a beer, and proceeds to tell the bartender a tale of woe. His aged and infirm parents had both taken a turn for the

[1]This article is a revised version of a keynote address to the 2nd International Congress on Integrative and Eclectic Psychotherapy, in Lyon, France, June 22, 1994. I am most grateful to Dr. John C. Norcross for presenting it on my behalf.
[2]Graduate School of Applied & Professional Psychology, Rutgers—The State University of New Jersey, New Brunswick, New Jersey.
[3]Correspondence should be directed to Arnold A. Lazarus, 56 Herrontown Circle, Princeton, New Jersey 08540-2924.

worse, and it was necessary to move them from Florida to a nursing home in New Jersey where their three children lived. This required several trips to and from Florida, negotiations with nursing home personnel, and the demanding process of cancelling the lease on their Florida apartment and storing and disposing of their possessions. Although he has a younger brother and sister, they willingly left all the work to him. His siblings both live no more than 10 or 15 minutes from the nursing home, but they seldom visit their parents, whereas he makes a point of seeing them at least four times a week. He has become increasingly annoyed with his sister and brother for their apparent lack of concern, and because they take for granted all that he has done and keeps on doing for their parents. His wife shares his resentment but also feels appalled that he has not insisted that his siblings share the burden. "I'm most unhappy about the situation," he says, "I feel angry, confused, upset and depressed."

The bartender, a high school dropout, offers him some advice. "I think, as the oldest brother," he says, "that you should tell them off and see to it that they pull their weight from now on." Has the bartender just dispensed some "psychotherapy?" Whatever we call it, this process—one human being telling another his or her troubles, expressing sadness and distress and receiving support or counsel in return—has probably occurred since time immemorial.

What if the bartender were a Rogerian therapist or person centered counselor moonlighting for extra income? Exuding empathy and warmth, he would presumably eschew advice giving but would reflect the patron's affective state. "I can hear how bothered you are," he might say, "how angry, confused, and upset you are." Would this be psychotherapy?

Perhaps a bartender well versed in family systems theory, might say, "It seems to me that you and your siblings are triangulated. As the eldest one, you play the role of the caretaker and do so with considerable martyrdom."

A rational-emotive bartender might point out that he is making himself upset and angry by virtue of the categorical imperatives to which he subscribes, and would probably inquire where it is written that his siblings should, ought, or must help out, or for that matter, why he had to visit his parents four times a week.

If the bartender happened to be a behavior therapist, perhaps he would stress the patron's basic lack of assertiveness and offer to do some role playing and behavior rehearsal.

And so it goes. The psychotherapist's orientation determines, to a large extent, how, what, when, why, and under which circumstances certain things are said or not said, and whether particular tactics are applied or withheld. The array of strategies invoked in the name of "psychotherapy" is vast.

The range extends from pensive listening to heroic pounding and screaming. But is there a right way, a best way to proceed? In our hypothetical example, would the untutored bartender's intervention prove any better or worse than his professionally trained counterparts? Strupp and Hadley (1979) were among the first to show that a group of professional therapists fared no better than sensitive and caring professors without any therapeutic training. But there is a catch.

TREATMENTS OF CHOICE

About 85% of people who are moderately anxious, frustrated, or distressed, mildly depressed, somewhat confused and unhappy, a little conflicted, and so forth, are likely to respond equally well to virtually any form of therapy, or they may recover from their afflictions without any formal therapy (Lambert, 1992). But this does not hold true for a variety of diagnostic categories such as most obsessive-compulsive disorders, eating disorders, posttraumatic stress disorders, panic disorders, sexual disorders, bipolar affective disorders, various personality disorders, schizophrenic disorders, and miscellaneous habit disorders. Likewise, the sufferers of most phobic conditions, those addicted to drugs or alcohol, and people who endure various forms of chronic pain fall into the category of patients who usually require specific *treatments of choice* if they are to be helped.

Thus, if a patient who suffers from agoraphobia receives insight-oriented therapy, or undergoes Jungian dream analysis, or is treated by intensive transactional analysis, a positive outcome (in terms of the client's freedom to travel about without anxiety) is unlikely unless some form of *exposure* is part of the treatment package (Freud, 1919). As Barlow (1988) stated, "investigators around the world have demonstrated very clearly that exposure *in vivo* is the central ingredient in the behavioral treatment of agoraphobia and that this process is substantially more effective than any number of credible alternative psychotherapeutic procedures" (p. 407). The point I am emphasizing is that practically any credible system of psychotherapy will assist many anxious or depressed neurotic patients, but specific treatments of choice are necessary for more disabling and refractory conditions. (Lazarus, 1991)

Therefore, when Mrs. W, a 28-year-old woman, complained that for the past year she had experienced overwhelming anxiety and panic when venturing away from home unless accompanied by her husband, one of the first lines of intervention, after history taking and the establishment of rapport, was graduated *in vivo* desensitization. She had completed the *Multi-*

modal Life History Inventory (Lazarus & Lazarus, 1991), which revealed several additional difficulties (e.g., marital discord, tensions between her and an older brother, feelings of resentment toward her parents, and issues pertaining to poor self-esteem and unassertiveness). I will use the case of Mrs. W to illustrate the virtues of technical eclecticism and to epitomize several of the traps of theoretical integration.

The first error that many therapists make is to assume that Mrs. W's other problems are *necessarily* connected to her agoraphobia. In fact, they may or may not be related. Her fears of travelling alone had been precipitated by a fainting spell in a shopping mall, presumably as the result of a viral infection. However, regardless of whether or not her marital and familial tensions had a direct or indirect bearing on her phobic avoidance, they needed remediation, as did her self-esteem issues and unassertiveness. But it is usually advisable to tackle first those problems that the client identifies as most salient. Consequently, she was taught relaxation and diaphragmatic breathing techniques, immediately followed by *in vivo* desensitization—in which we first took short walks followed by longer drives, gradually increasing the distance between us. The patient's husband was included in the therapy because spousal involvement appears to enhance treatment outcomes (Barlow, 1993; Carter, Turovsky, & Barlow, 1994).

At this juncture there was no need for eclecticism or integration. The methods employed followed the mandates of scientific discovery, which suggest that behavioral interventions are strongly indicated (e.g., Barlow, 1988; Wolpe, 1958, 1990). But when, during and after several *in vivo* excursions, Mrs. W related disturbing flashbacks to real or imagined memories (such as undue parental censure, upsetting images of peer rejection and humiliation, and a sense of having been abandoned) it seemed advisable to expand the treatment repertoire. Once again, it must be stressed that these additional problems may or may not have had a bearing on her agoraphobia. Nevertheless, when further problems are identified, it makes sense to address them.

Initially, a form of role playing was employed in which Mrs. W attempted to confront her father about certain resentments she had harbored. When she implied that I was not capturing or conveying the essence of her father's tone and demeanor correctly, we switched from role playing to the two-chair or empty-chair technique. Now, while first speaking to the empty chair in which she envisioned her father sitting, and then moving to that chair, becoming her father, and talking for him, she achieved a feeling of greater authenticity. This was reflected in considerable emotionality—what she herself termed "cathartic release."

SOME OF THE TRAPS

When introducing the empty-chair technique, it could be argued that the treatment had become "eclectic" or "integrative." First of all, we were now addressing memories from the past (which is what psychoanalysts do); second, we had drawn on a method (the empty-chair technique) that originated in gestalt therapy and psychodrama circles. Subsequently, when Mrs. W related her sense of abandonment to a "forgotten memory" in which, when she was almost 4 years old, her mother, who had to undergo surgery, had sent her to live with foster parents for several weeks, we seemed to be venturing even deeper into psychodynamic territory. Let us now address several points of potential confusion.

In my opinion, it is an egregious error to assert that in addition to behavior therapy, I was now practicing gestalt therapy, psychodrama, and psychodynamic psychotherapy. I had borrowed techniques from different disciplines but had remained firmly within the purview of social and cognitive learning theory (e.g., Bandura, 1986). This *technical eclecticism* (Lazarus, 1967, 1989, 1992; Lazarus, Beutler, & Norcross, 1992; Lazarus & Beutler, 1993) permits one to select techniques from any discipline without necessarily endorsing any of the theories that spawned them. The trap lies in equating observations with theories (Lazarus, 1993b). For example, I may *observe* that someone is displacing anger or denying his or her rage, but to do so does not mean that I am thereby endorsing any psychodynamic *theories vis-à-vis* so-called defense mechanisms.

Thus, when Mrs. W was recounting her childhood memories, dwelling on the affective pain she experienced while separated from her mother at age 4, and linking these emotions to present-day perceptions, this may have looked and sounded like psychoanalytic or psychodynamic therapy, but it was decidedly different for the following reasons:

1. My theoretical understanding of the processes did not invoke Oedipal issues, the nuances of object relations, drive/structural or ego psychology models, or rest on any other psychodynamic assumptions. Instead, I viewed her reactions in terms of a broad-based social learning theory with its attendant associations, positive and negative reinforcers, cognitive contingencies, expectancies, extinction paradigms, and so forth. Certainly, there was no need or attempt to blend behavioral and psychodynamic theories.
2. My clinical treatment of the material differed significantly from psychodynamic practitioners. In Mrs. W's case, one of the

techniques I employed on several occasions was *time tripping*, in which I had her imagine herself using a "time machine" to go back to the past, to visit her alter ego at age 4. Thus, the 28-year-old Mrs. W talked to her 4-year-old counterpart, offered the child support, love, solace, understanding, and encouragement. (I view this as a variant of cognitive restructuring and desensitization. It tends to neutralize patients to memories of their past hurts and tends to free them from the shackles of their negative childhood encounters.) Moreover, Mrs. W was encouraged to employ self-talk. She was advised, "Whenever you experience these feelings of abandonment, take a deep breath, then exhale slowly, relax and say to yourself over and over again: 'I am not 4 years old. I'm an adult. I can and do feel secure.' Stand tall when you say this to yourself and feel your power and maturity." Psychodynamic therapists would treat Mrs. W very differently.

Similarly, I am practicing neither gestalt therapy nor psychodrama when employing the empty-chair technique because both my rationale for so doing and the manner in which it is administered differs significantly from its original format and intent. And yet, when discussing the foregoing clinical strategies with certain colleagues, they would assert that I was a "closet analyst" or had indeed practiced "gestalt therapy." What I had actually done was to borrow some techniques from different disciplines, incorporate them into my own theoretical framework, and in so doing, change them into something different from the way they were conceived and applied within their original paradigm (Lazarus & Messer, 1991).

ONE OF THE BIGGEST MISCONCEPTIONS

A typical refrain among integrationists is, "I use psychodynamic psychotherapy with some patients, behavior therapy with others, or I may draw from both with the same patient at different stages." Rhoads (1984) and Wachtel (1977, 1991) exemplify the foregoing view. However, in my estimation, they have blended phenotypical elements and bypassed the genotypical differences that truly underlie these two fundamentally different orientations. Indeed, at this genotypical and primary level, how is it possible to blend two systems that rest on totally different assumptions about the meaning, origins, development, maintenance, significance, and management of problems? Strictly speaking, it is impossible to achieve a truly basic psychodynamic-behavioral blend (see Franks, 1984), but let us see how certain issues become fused and confused in practice. (Again, let me emphasize that one may use *techniques* from different schools while remaining theoretically consistent—see Dryden, 1987.)

One of my patients, who suffered from a generalized anxiety disorder, appeared to be overprotesting the purity of his motives behind a business merger that earned him considerable money at the expense of his partner. He described dreams in which his partner either attacked him in person or hired others to inflict bodily harm. His associations to these dreams reinforced his belief that his partner had, in fact, always been antagonistic to him. He denied having feelings of guilt and proceeded to rationalize that, because of his partner's alleged hostility to him, he had done nothing improper. Upon further reflection, he got in touch with several emotions that he had often experienced as a child. He vividly recounted how his older brother had bullied and intimidated him, and he subsequently drew a parallel between his brother and his partner. "I never realized until now how much Charles [his partner] reminds me of Harold [his brother]." A little later, he ventured to suggest that he may very well have been getting back at Harold by undermining Charles—"his psychic look-alike."

The foregoing paragraph alludes to several psychotherapeutic processes that served to elicit information of which the patient was unaware and that enabled him to make some seemingly important connections between past and present feelings. He got beyond certain rationalizations and denials and gained insight into possible motives behind his behavior. Was I administering psychodynamic therapy? In my opinion, I was not. I was using, for want of a better term, *applied psychology*. To apply methods that bear some resemblance to procedures that psychodynamic therapists employ does not translate into "doing psychodynamic psychotherapy." When one recognizes and treats certain defensive reactions, and delves into different levels of awareness (nonconscious processes), one does not need to muddy the issues by drawing on or operating from a psychodynamic perspective. Such concepts as "nonconscious processes" and "defensive reactions" are well documented, in a very different manner from the psychodynamic context, in the areas of social and experimental psychology (Lazarus, 1989). They differ from the way in which psychodynamic theorists underwrite specific theories of unconscious motivation. For example, in the aforementioned case, a complete psychodynamic explanation of the client's sibling rivalry would undoubtedly rest on putative concepts of "object relations," "ego development," and so forth. Psychodynamic theorists would make many other inferences and interpretations that go far beyond the social and cognitive learning theory framework that I endorse. And in so doing, they would espouse notions that are not capable of scientific verification or disproof.

The point I am trying to emphasize is that one does not have to resort to any psychoanalytic or psychodynamic theories when recognizing that there are often more to things than meets the eye, when reading between the lines, or uncovering hidden meanings or symbolic events. One of my colleagues remarked that he was treating a heterosexual man who was obsessed with and inordinately afraid of contracting AIDS. "To be psychodynamic," he said, "I wonder whether his fear of AIDS is really a fear of being homosexual." Why is this "being psychodynamic?" In terms of "stimulus generalization" and various "semantic differentials," one may postulate a hierarchy of primary and secondary fears (Osgood, 1953). Indeed, upon discussing the matter with my colleague, he stated quite emphatically that he rejected all three of the most influential psychodynamic approaches—structural theory, self-psychology, and object relations theory. So how was he "being psychodynamic?" As already mentioned, one may refer to levels of awareness, nonconscious processes, and defensive reactions without buying into any "psychodynamic" explications.[4] To refer to any form of psychologizing as "being psychodynamic" only confuses the issue. An article by Scaturo (1994) provides an exemplary opportunity to underscore this assertion.

In treating panic disorder and agoraphobia, Scaturo argues for a combination of cognitive-behavioral procedures and psychoanalytically oriented therapy. He commences with basic behavioral methods such as relaxation training, diaphragmatic breathing, exposure, and cognitive restructuring, and then states, "My own clinical work with patients presenting with panic disorder has led me to believe that abandonment and separation anxiety are the primary sources of anxiety for these patients" (p. 260). (Is this true for 100% of patients presenting with panic disorder, or could it apply perhaps to a much smaller percentage?) But I emphatically disagree with Scaturo's belief that panic disorder, indeed all problems, are "strongly linked to psychodynamic origins" (p. 256). In my view, a social-cognitive learning theory adequately accounts for panic disorder and all other psychological problems without resorting to notions drawn from object-relations theory, or any other psychodynamic perspective.

Due to his basic psychoanalytic leanings, Scaturo, after treating panic disorder behaviorally, believes it necessary for patients to achieve an understanding of historical antecedents. This is his *bias*. But let us assume that he has proof that behavior therapy *plus* exploratory psychotherapy

---

[4]When I refer to "levels of awareness," I am not talking about Freudian concepts of conscious, preconscious, and unconscious minds. Nor do "nonconscious processes" have any bearing on "the unconscious" with its putative complexes and intrapsychic functions. The "psychological unconscious" (see Shevrin & Dickman, 1980) is very different from the Freudian or neo-Freudian unconscious.

yields more durable outcomes. Why must "exploration" necessarily be "psychodynamic?" Note how in my account of Mrs. W, the nonpsychodynamic assessment unearthed significant historical factors (including separation anxiety at age 4). Was this "separation anxiety" necessarily related to her panic attacks? And was it, as Scaturo would allege, "the core interpersonal issue of [her] panic symptoms" (p. 260). In my view, it was not. Nevertheless, in her case, because the multimodal (not psychoanalytic) exploration had revealed an event of "separation anxiety," this was addressed and apparently resolved via time tripping and simple positive self-affirmation (and was not handled psychodynamically).

Scaturo provides a case vignette that purports to show his behavioral-psychodynamic blend. Mrs. A (who had initially failed to respond to psychoanalytic therapy) closely resembles my case of Mrs. W. Our respective treatments coincided on most fronts, and I detected nothing that I would label "psychoanalytic" in Scaturo's brief write-up. Nevertheless, he insists that he achieved "a synergism between behavioral and psychodynamic interventions" (p. 269). It is this penchant in many quarters of labeling any form of inquiry into the past as "psychoanalytic" or "psychodynamic," and giving this same label to any type of insight or self-understanding, that simply muddies the waters and results in the needless attempt to blend two fundamentally incompatible paradigms. As I have argued for many years (Lazarus, 1976, 1989, 1992), a multimodal assessment that evaluates a client's behaviors, affective reactions, sensations, images, cognitions, interpersonal relationships, and biological processes, typically reveals a matrix of discrete and interrelated problems—both intrapersonal and contextual—that facilitates clinical attention to a wide array of salient issues. But one's essential base of operations remains firmly within the framework of a social cognitive theory (Bandura 1986) without resorting to notions from any other theoretical system (but with the freedom to import effective techniques at will).

WHAT CAN BE INTEGRATED?

I have three patients scheduled—one at 2 pm, another at 3 pm, and a third at 4 pm. When seeing my first client, I say very little. He dwells on childhood memories and I listen attentively. Occasionally, I may ask a question—"Did you feel any anger at the time?" or "Do you see a connection between this event and the way you tend to protect yourself from criticism?" Now and then I may make a comment or share an observation. (I do not make interpretations—you do or feel x because of y—because interpretations strike me as presumptuous.) Thus, I may say, "It seems to me that your sexual insecurity is possibly linked to that adolescent memory" or "I'm not so sure that your mother necessarily wanted you to believe that." My comments are open for discussion—if the client disagrees with me, he or she is not necessarily resisting. I see a world of difference between psychodynamic interpretations and behaviorally based interpretive suggestions. Yet, if someone who knew nothing about me or my orientation viewed a videotape of that session, he or she would probably conclude that I was a practicing analyst, or certainly a psychodynamic psychotherapist.

By contrast, with my 3 pm client, I am very active and disputational, energetically parsing dysfunctional beliefs, and often resorting to a form of Socratic questioning. An observer would probably conclude that I was some type of "cognitive therapist."

My 4 pm client is kept busy rehearsing two important upcoming life events—what speech to make at a prize-winning ceremony where she will receive her firm's annual award as the most creative designer, and how to approach her mother assertively, rather than timidly or aggressively, about an unresolved altercation. The role playing and social skills training techniques would immediately clearly place me in the behavioral camp.

The point I wish to make here is that I was not practicing psychodynamic therapy at 2 pm, cognitive therapy at 3, and behavior therapy at 4. Rather, I was employing listening and reflecting *techniques* at 2, cognitive restructuring *techniques* at 3, and behavior rehearsal *techniques* at 4. The techniques I selected were in keeping with my perceptions of the clients' specific needs and expectancies, plus evidence that salubrious results were emanating from my different ministrations. As a technical eclectic, I can use operant techniques or psychoanalytic techniques without subscribing to the theories that gave rise to the methods I employ. I would not be integrating any *theoretical* viewpoints; rather, as I see it, at all times, I would be operating out of a broad-based social cognitive learning framework.

I have emphasized for many years that a blend of different theories is likely to result only in profound confusion. Too many seemingly compatible ideas are, upon closer scrutiny, quite irreconcilable. Furthermore, I am not aware of a single instance wherein a blend of different theories produced a more powerful technique. But, to reiterate, I am familiar with many instances in which the selection of *techniques* from different disciplines has enriched clinicians' armamentaria. (Anyone wishing to appreciate the extent of *heterogeneity* that prevails throughout the field of psychotherapy integration might want to read Norcross and Goldfried's, 1992, excellent handbook.)

But the term "integration" does not have to refer solely to attempts at a theoretical amalgamation. One might argue, that for some patients, the integration of individual and group therapy will prove beneficial. For others, the integration of psychosocial therapy and drug therapy may be strongly indicated. If so-called integrationists focused on the application of different *treatment combinations*, progress is more likely to ensue. This may result in more attention to factors and processes that genuinely facilitate therapeutic change—matching the appropriate selection of *techniques* with different *relationship styles* (Beutler & Clarkin, 1990; Lazarus, 1993a). As Wolpe (1994, personal communication) has emphasized, "The important question is not what theory you believe but what empirical warrant there is for the efficacy of particular psychotherapeutic behavior."

A BRIEF COMMENT ON COMMON FACTORS

As Arkowitz (1989) and Norcross and Newman (1992) have underscored, there are *three routes to integration*—technical eclecticism, theoretical integration, and common factors. As I have emphasized, I strongly favor technical eclecticism and regard theoretical integration with considerable suspicion if not disdain. Because I also have some misgivings about the common factors approach, for the sake of completeness, I will make some brief comments about common factors.

The common factors approach seeks to determine the core ingredients shared by different therapies. Considerable attention has been devoted to identifying common or unifying themes across disparate systems of psychotherapy. The chief proponents of this approach (e.g., Beitman, 1987; Frank, 1982; Garfield, 1992; Goldfried, 1982) have identified various healing processes—be it increased self-efficacy, enhanced morale, corrective emotional experiences, various forms of feedback, or the power of the therapeutic alliance.

To identify common factors may prove somewhat useful, if by so doing, we can discover the *active ingredients* that lead to positive gains. Let's assume, for instance, that Frank (1982) has correctly identified *enhanced morale* as the basis for virtually all successful psychotherapeutic outcomes. The question nevertheless remains: How do we best go about achieving this worthy end? So my thesis is that common factors *per se* do not tell us very much. We still require systematic research into crucial similarities and essential differences.

The overriding question to my way of thinking is how best to evaluate clinical experience and propose new ways of explaining or treating human suffering. Nuland (1994) recommends the following: "(1) meticulous and personally made observations of an illness or maladaptive state; (2) evenhanded review of all pertinent publications that bear on the problem; (3) scrupulous attention to every fragment of clinical evidence, whether or not it supports the observer's evolving hypothesis; and (4) a commitment not to speculate beyond what is justified by the accumulated data and its supportable implications" (p. 4). Far too many enthusiastic researchers and practitioners are naive about the ways of serious research and are too eager to forgo the constraints that govern the objective evaluation of evidence. Premature integration may result in clinical disintegration!

I see the major guiding principle to effective psychotherapy as a slight modification of Gordon Paul's (1967) profound directive: *What* treatment, by *whom*, is most effective for *this* individual, with *those* specific problems, and under *which* set of circumstances? It is impossible to embrace this dictum and yet remain within the boundaries of any delimited school of thought. Serious consideration of what-is-truly-best-for-this-individual (or for these individuals in the case of couples, families, and groups) should free us from the shackles of our training and superstitions and enable us to be of far-reaching service to the people who ask us for help.

ACKNOWLEDGMENTS

My thanks to Hal Arkowitz and an anonymous referee for their trenchant criticisms of my initial draft. I actually incorporated a few of the changes they recommended!

REFERENCES

Arkowitz, H. (1989). The role of theory in psychotherapy integration. *Journal of Integrative and Eclectic Psychotherapy, 8,* 8-16.

Bandura, A. (1986). *Social foundations of thought and action: A social cognitive theory.* Englewood Cliffs, NJ: Prentice-Hall.

Barlow, D. H. (1988). *Anxiety and its disorders.* New York: Guilford Press.

Barlow, D. H. (1993). Implications of clinical research for psychotherapy integration in the treatment of the anxiety disorders. *Journal of Psychotherapy Integration, 3,* 297-311.

Beitman, B. D. (1987). *The structure of individual psychotherapy.* New York: Guilford.

Beutler, L. E., & Clarkin, J. F. (1990). *Systematic treatment selection: Toward targeted therapeutic interventions.* New York: Brunner/Mazel.

Carter, M. M., Turovsky, J., & Barlow, D. H. (1994). Interpersonal relationships in panic disorder with agoraphobia: A review of empirical evidence. *Clinical Psychology: Science and Practice, 1,* 25-34.

Dryden, W. (1987). Theoretically consistent eclecticism: Humanizing a computer "addict." In J. C. Norcross (Ed.). *Casebook of eclectic psychotherapy* (pp. 221-237). New York: Brunner/Mazel.

Frank, J. D. (1982). Therapeutic components shared by all psychotherapies. In J. H. Harvey & M. M. Parks (Eds.), *The Master Lecture Series: Vol. 1. Psychotherapy research and behavior change* (pp. 73-122). Washington, DC: American Psychological Association.

Franks, C. M. (1984). On conceptual and technical integrity in psychoanalysis and behavior therapy: Two fundamentally incompatible systems. In H. Arkowitz & S. B. Messer (Eds.),

Psychoanalytic therapy and behavior therapy: Is integration possible? (pp. 223-247). New York: Plenum Press.

Freud, S. (1919). Turnings in the ways of psychoanalytic therapy. *Collected Papers* (Vol. 2). London: Hogarth.

Garfield, S. L. (1992). Eclectic psychotherapy: A common factors approach. In J. C. Norcross & M. R. Goldfried (Eds.), *Handbook of psychotherapy integration* (pp. 169-201). New York: Basic Books.

Goldfried, M. R. (Ed.) (1982). *Converging themes in psychotherapy*. New York: Springer.

Lambert, M. J. (1992). Psychotherapy outcome research: Implications for integrative and eclectic therapists. In J. C. Norcross & M. R. Goldfried (Eds.), *Handbook of psychotherapy integration* (pp. 94-129). New York: Basic Books.

Lazarus, A. A. (1967). In support of technical eclecticism. *Psychological Reports*, *21*, 415-416.

Lazarus, A. A. (1976). *Multimodal behavior therapy*. New York: Springer.

Lazarus, A. A. (1989). *The practice of multimodal therapy*. Baltimore, MD: Johns Hopkins University Press.

Lazarus, A. A. (1991). A plague on Little Hans and Little Albert. *Psychotherapy*, *28*, 444-447.

Lazarus, A. A. (1992). Multimodal therapy: Technical eclecticism with minimal integration. In J. C. Norcross & M. R. Goldfried (Eds.), *Handbook of psychotherapy integration* (pp. 231-263). New York: Basic Books.

Lazarus, A. A. (1993a). Tailoring the therapeutic relationship, or being an authentic chameleon. *Psychotherapy*, *30*, 404-407.

Lazarus, A. A. (1993b). Theory, subjectivity and bias: Can there be a future? *Psychotherapy*, *30*, 674-677.

Lazarus, A. A., & Lazarus, C. N. (1991). *Multimodal Life History Inventory*. Champaign, IL: Research Press.

Lazarus, A. A., & Messer, S. B. (1991). Does chaos prevail? An exchange on technical eclecticism and assimilative integration. *Journal of Psychotherapy Integration*, *1*, 143-158.

Lazarus, A. A., Beutler, L. E., & Norcross, J. C. (1992). The future of technical eclecticism. *Psychotherapy*, *29*, 11-20.

Lazarus, A. A., & Beutler, L. E. (1993). On technical eclecticism. *Journal of Counseling & Development*, *71*, 381-385.

Norcross, J. C., & Goldfried, M. R. (Eds.) (1992). *Handbook of psychotherapy integration*. New York: Basic Books.

Norcross, J. C., & Newman, C. F. (1992). Psychotherapy integration: Setting the context. In J. C. Norcross & M. R. Goldfried (Eds.). *Handbook of psychotherapy integration* (pp. 3-45). New York: Basic Books.

Nuland, S. B. (1994). The pill of pills. *The New York Review of Books*, *51*, 4-8.

Osgood (1953). *Method and theory in experimental psychology*. London: Oxford University Press.

Paul, G. L. (1967). Strategy of outcome research in psychotherapy. *Journal of Consulting Psychology*, *31*, 109-118.

Rhoads, J. M. (1984). Relationship between psychodynamic and behavior therapies. In H. Arkowitz & S. B. Messer (Eds.), *Psychoanalytic therapy and behavior therapy: Is integration possible?* (pp. 195-211). New York: Plenum Press.

Scaturo, D. J. (1994). Integrative psychotherapy for panic disorder and agoraphobia in clinical practice. *Journal of Psychotherapy Integration*, *4*, 253-272.

Shevrin, H., & Dickman, S. (1980). The psychological unconscious: A necessary assumption for all psychological theory? *American Psychologist*, *35*, 421-434.

Strupp, H. H., & Hadley, S. W. (1979). Specific versus nonspecific factors in psychotherapy. *Archives of General Psychiatry*, *36*, 1125-1136.

Wachtel, P. L. (1977). *Psychoanalysis and behavior therapy: Toward an integration*. New York: Basic Books.

Wachtel, P. L. (1991). From eclecticism to synthesis: Toward a more seamless psycho-therapeutic integration. *Journal of Psychotherapy Integration*, *1*, 43-54.

Wolpe, J. (1958). *Psychotherapy by reciprocal inhibition*. Stanford, CA: Stanford University Press.

Wolpe, J. (1990). *The practice of behavior therapy* (4th ed.). New York: Pergamon Press.

References

Anderson, T. (1992). Thoughts on the nature of the therapeutic relationship. In J. S. Rutan (Ed.), *Psychotherapy for the 1990s.* New York: Guilford.

Arkowitz, H. (1989). The role of theory in psychotherapy integration. *Journal of Integrative and Eclectic Psychotherapy, 8,* 8–16.

Bach, G. R., & Wyden, P. (1969). *The intimate enemy.* New York: Morrow.

Bandura, A. (1986). *Social foundations of thought and action.* Englewood Cliffs, NJ: Prentice-Hall.

Barlow, D. H. (1988). *Anxiety and its disorders.* New York: Guilford.

Barlow, D. H., & Cerny, J. A. (1988). *Psychological treatment of panic.* New York: Guilford.

Barlow, D. H., & Craske, M. G. (1989). *Mastery of your anxiety and panic.* Albany, NY: Graywind.

Barzun, J. (1986). *A word or two before you go. . . .* Middletown, CT: Wesleyan University Press.

Beck, A.T. (1991). Cognitive therapy: A 30-year retrospective. *American Psychologist, 46,* 368–375.

Bemporad, J. R. (1995). Individual psychotherapy. In I .D. Glick (Ed.), *Treating depression.* San Francisco: Jossey-Bass.

Berenbaum, H. (1969). Massed time-limited psychotherapy. *Psychotherapy: Theory, Research and Practice, 6,* 54–56.

Beutler, L. E. , Consoli, A. J., & Williams, R. E. (1995). Integrative and eclectic therapies in practice. In B. Bongar & L. E. Beutler (Eds.), *Comprehensive textbook of psychotherapy.* New York: Oxford University Press.

Borys, D. S. (1994). Maintaining therapeutic boundaries: The motive is therapeutic effectiveness, not defensive practice. *Ethics and Behavior, 4,* 267–273.

Budman, S. H. (Ed.) (1981). *Forms of brief therapy.* New York: Guilford.

Budman, S. H. (Ed.) (1995). *Forms of brief therapy.* (Update) New York: Guilford.

Budman, S. H. (1994). *Treating time effectively: The first session In brief therapy.* New York: Guilford.

Budman, S. H., & Gurman, A. S. (1988). *Theory and practice of brief therapy.* New York: Guilford.

Carter, M. M., Turovsky, J., & Barlow, D. H. (1994). Interpersonal relationships in panic disorder with agoraphobia. *Clinical Psychology: Science and Practice, 1,* 25–34.

Chambless, D. (1955). Training in and dissemination of empirically validated psychological treatments: Report and recommendations. *The Clinical Psychologist, 48,* 3–23.

Cooper, J. F. (1995). *A primer of brief psychotherapy.* New York: Norton.

165

Craighead, W. E. (1990). There's a place for us all: All of us. *Behavior Therapy, 21,*3–23.

Crews, F. (1986). *Skeptical engagements.* New York: Oxford University Press.

Cummings, N. A. (1985). The dismantling of our health care system: Strategies for the survival of psychological practice. *American Psychologist, 41,* 426–431.

Cummings, N. A. (1988). Emergence of the mental health complex: Adaptive and maladaptive responses. *Professional Psychology, 19,* 308–315.

Cummings, N. A. (1991). The somatizing patient. In C. S. Austad & W. H. Berman (Eds.), *Psychotherapy in managed health care: The optimal use of time and resources.* Washington, D.C.: American Psychological Association.

Cummings, N. A., & Sayama, M. (1995). *Focused psychotherapy.* New York: Brunner/Mazel.

Davanloo, H. (Ed.) (1978). *Basic principles and techniques in short-term dynamic psychotherapy.* New York: Spectrum.

Davison, G. C., & Lazarus, A. A. (1994). Clinical innovation and evaluation: Integrating practice with inquiry. *Clinical Psychology: Science and Practice, 1,* 157–168.

Davison, G. C., & Lazarus, A. A. (1995). The dialectics of science and practice. In S. C. Hayes, V. M. Foulette, R. M. Dawes, & K. E. Grady (Eds.), *Scientific standards of psychological practice: Issues and recommendations.* Reno, NV: Context.

de Shazer, S. (1988). *Clues: Investigating solutions in brief therapy.* New York: Norton.

Dreiblatt, I. S., & Weatherly, D. (1965). An evaluation of the efficacy of brief contact therapy with hospitalized psychiatric patients. *Journal of Consulting Psychology, 29,* 513–519.

Dryden, W. (1995). *Brief rational-emotive behaviour therapy.* Chichester: Wiley.

Ellis, A. (1962). *Reason and emotion in psychotherapy.* New York: Lyle Stuart.

Ellis, A. (1994). *Reason and emotion in psychotherapy* (Revised). New York: Birch Lane.

Ellis, A. (1996). *Better, deeper and more eduring brief therapy.* New York: Brunner/Mazel.

Fairburn, C. G. (1993). *Interpersonal psychotherapy for bulimia nervosa.* Washington, DC: American Psychiatric Association.

Fay, A. (1994). *PQR: Prescription for a quality relationship.* San Luis Obispo, CA: Impact.

Fay, A. (1995). Boundaries in the physician-patient relationship. *Journal of theAmerican Medical Association, 274,* 1345–1346.

Fay, A., & Lazarus, A. A. (1993). On necessity and sufficiency in psychotherapy. *Psychotherapy in Private Practice, 12,* 33–39.

Frankl, V. (1967). *Psychotherapy and existentialism.* New York: Simon & Schuster.

Franks, C. M. (1982). Behavior therapy: An overview. In C. M. Franks, G. T. Wilson , P. C. Kendall, & K. D. Brownell (Eds.), *Annual Review of Behavior Therapy: Theory and Practice,* Vol. 8. New York: Guilford.

Franks, C. M. (1984). On conceptual and technical integrity in psychoanalysis and behavior therapy: Two fundamentally incompatible systems. In H. Arkowitz & S. B. Messer (Eds.), *Psychoanalytic therapy and behavior therapy: Is integration possible?* New York: Plenum.

Gabbard, G. O., & Nadelson, C. (1995a). Professional boundaries in the physician- patient relationship. *Journal of the American Medical Association, 273,* 1445–449.

Gabbard, G. O., & Nadelson, C. (1995b). In reply. *Journal of the American Medical Association, 274,* 1346.

Gergen, K. J. (1982). *Toward transformation in social knowledge.* New York: Springer-Verlag.

Goldfried, M. R., & Davison, G. C. (1994). *Clinical behavior therapy.* (Expanded Edition). New York: Wiley.

Goodkin, B. (1981). *A therapist's notebook.* Little Falls, NJ: Lennox.

Gottman, J. (1994) *Why marriages succeed or fail.* New York: Simon & Schuster.

Gutheil, T. G. (1989). Patient-therapist sexual relations. *Harvard Medical School Mental Health Letter, 6,* 4–6.

Gutheil, T. G. (1994). Discussion of Lazarus's "How certain boundaries and ethics diminish therapeutic effectiveness." *Ethics and Behavior, 4,* 295–298.

Haley, J. (1993). *Jay Haley on Milton H. Erickson.* New York: Brunner/Mazel.

Heide, F. J., & Borkovec, T. D. (1983). Relaxation-induced anxiety: Paradoxical anxiety enhancement due to relaxation training. *Journal of Consulting and Clinical Psychology, 51,* 171–182.

Heide, F. J., & Borkovec, T. D. (1984). Relaxation-induced anxiety: Mechanisms and theoretical implications. *Behaviour Research and Therapy, 22,* 1–12.

Held, B. S. (1995). *Back to reality: A critique of postmodern theory in psychotherapy.* New York: Norton.

Herman, S. M. (1991). Client-therapist similarity on the Multimodal Structural Profile as predictive of psychotherapy outcome. *Psychotherapy Bulletin, 26,* 26–27.

Herman, S. M. (1991a). A psychometric evaluation of the Marital Satisfaction Questionnaire: A demonstration of reliability and validity. *Psychotherapy in Private Practice, 9,* 85–94.

Herman, S. M. (1992). Client-therapist similarity on the Multimodal Structural Profile as predictive of psychotherapy outcome. Doctoral dissertation, Department of Psychology, Rutgers University.

Herman, S. M. (1993). A demonstration of the validity of the Multimodal Structural Profile through a correlation with the Vocational Preference Inventory. *Psychotherapy in Private Practice, 11,* 71–80.

Hersen, M., & Ammerman, R. T. (Eds.) (1994). *Handbook of prescriptive treatments for adults.* New York: Plenum.

Horney, K. (1950). *Neurosis and human growth: The struggle toward self-realization.* New York: Norton.

Howard, K. I., Kopta, S. M., Krause, M. S., & Orlinski, D. E. (1986). The dose-effect relationship in psychotherapy. *American Psychologist, 41,* 159–164.

Howard, G. S., Nance, D. W., & Myers, P. (1987). *Adaptive counseling and therapy.* San Francisco: Jossey-Bass.

Hoyt, M. F. (1989). On time in brief therapy. In R. Wells & V. Gianetti (Eds.), *Handbook of brief psychotherapies.* New York: Plenum.

Hoyt, M. F. (1995). *Brief therapy and managed care.* San Francisco: Jossey-Bass.

Karasu, T. B. (1992). *Wisdom in the practice of psychotherapy.* New York: Basic.

Karpel, M. A. (1994). *Evaluating couples: A handbook for practitioners.* New York: Norton.

Katzenbach, J. R. (1995). *Real change leaders.* New York: Times Business (Random House).

Kazdin, A. E. (1984). Integration of psychodynamic and behavioral psychotherapies: Conceptual Versus Empirical Synthesis. In H. Arkowitz, & S. B. Messer (Eds.), *Psychoanalytic therapy and behavior therapy: Is integration possible?* New York: Basic.

Kazdin, A. E. (1996). Combined and multimodal treatments in child and adolescent psychotherapy: Issues, challenges, and research directions. *Clinical Psychology: Science and Practice, 3,* 69–100.

Kellermann, P. F. (1992). *Focus on psychodrama.* Philadelphia: Jessica Kingsley.

Kennedy, R. (1976). Self-induced depersonalization syndrome. *American Journal of Psychiatry, 133,* 1326–1328.

Klerman, G. L., Weissman, M. M., Rounsaville, B. J., & Chevron, E. S. (1984). *Interpersonal psychotherapy of depression.* New York: Basic.

Koegler, R. R., & Cannon, J. A. (1966). Treatment for the many. In G. J. Wayne &. R. R. Koegler (Eds.), *Emergency psychiatry and brief therapy*. Boston: Little, Brown.

Kopp, R. R. (1995). *Metaphor therapy*. New York: Brunner/Mazel.

Kopta, S. M., Howard, K. I., Lowry, J. L., & Beutler, L. E. (1994). Patterns of symptomatic recovery in psychotherapy. *Journal of Consulting and Clinical Psychology, 62*, 1009–1016.

Kwee, M. G. T. (1996) Personal communication.

Kwee, M. G. T., & Holdstock, T. L. (1996). (Eds.). *Western and Buddhist psychology: Clinical perspectives.* Delft: Eburon.

Kwee, M. G. T., & Lazarus, A. A. (1986). Multimodal therapy: The cognitive- behavioral tradition and beyond. In W. Dryden & W. Golden (Eds.), *Cognitive-behavioral approaches to psychotherapy*. London: Harper & Row.

Lambert, M. J. (1992). Psychotherapy outcome research: Implications for integrative and eclectic therapists. In J. C.. Norcross & M. R. Goldfried (Eds.), *Handbook of psychotherapy integration*. New York: Basic.

Landes, A. A. (1988). Assessment of the reliability and validity of the Multimodal Structural Profile Inventory. Doctoral Dissertation, Graduate School of Applied and Professional Psychology, Rutgers University.

Landes, A. A. (1991). Development of the Structural Profile Inventory. *Psychotherapy in Private Practice, 9*, 123–141.

Lazarus, A. A. (1956). A psychological approach to alcoholism. *South African Medical Journal, 30*, 707–710.

Lazarus, A. A. (1965). Towards the understanding and effective treatment of alcoholism. *South African Medical Journal, 39*, 736–741.

Lazarus, A. A. (1967). In support of technical eclecticism. *Psychological Reports, 21*, 415–516.

Lazarus, A. A. (1968). Learning theory and the treatment of depression. *Behaviour Research and Therapy, 6*, 83–89.

Lazarus, A. A. (1969). Broad-spectrum behavior therapy. *Newsletter of the Association for Advancement of Behavior Therapy, 4*, 5–6.

Lazarus, A. A. (1971). *Behavior therapy and beyond*. New York: McGraw-Hill. (Reissued by Jason Aronson, with updated preface, 1996.)

Lazarus, A. A. (1973). Multimodal behavior therapy: Treating the BASIC ID. *Journal of Nervous and Mental Disease, 156*, 404–411.

Lazarus, A. A. (1976). *Multimodal behavior therapy*. New York: Springer Publishing.

Lazarus, A. A. (1976a). Psychiatric problems precipitated by transcendental meditation. *Psychological Reports, 39*, 601–602.

Lazarus, A. A. (1977). Toward an egoless state of being. In A. Ellis & R. Grieger (Eds.), *Handbook of rational-emotive therapy*. New York: Springer Publishing.

Lazarus, A. A. (1981). *The practice of multimodal therapy*. New York: McGraw-Hill.

Lazarus, A. A. (1984). *In the mind's eye*. New York: Guilford.

Lazarus, A. A. (1985). *Marital myths*. San Luis Obispo, CA: Impact.

Lazarus, A. A. (1989). *The practice of multimodal therapy* (Update). Baltimore: Johns Hopkins University Press.

Lazarus, A. A. (1989a). Why I am an eclectic (not an integrationist). *British Journal of Guidance and Counselling, 17*, 248–258.

Lazarus, A. A. (1989b). The practice of rational-emotive therapy. In M. E. Bernard., & R. DiGiuseppe (Eds.), *Inside rational-emotive therapy*. New York: Academic.

Lazarus, A. A. (1992). When is couples therapy necessary and sufficient? *Psychological Reports,* *70*, 787–790.

Lazarus, A. A. (1993). Tailoring the therapeutic relationship, or being an authentic chameleon. *Psychotherapy, 30,* 404–407.

Lazarus, A. A. (1994). How certain boundaries and ethics diminish therapeutic effectiveness. *Ethics & Behavior, 4,* 255–261.

Lazarus, A. A. (1995). Different types of eclecticism and integration: Let's be aware of the dangers. *Journal of Psychotherapy Integration, 5,* 27–39.

Lazarus, A. A. (1995a). Adjusting the carburetor: Pivotal clinical interventions in marital and sex therapy. In R. C. Rosen & S. R. Leiblum (Eds.), *Case studies in sex therapy.* New York: Guilford.

Lazarus, A. A. (1996). The utility and futility of combining treatments in psychotherapy. *Clinical Psychology: Science and Practice, 3,* 59–68.

Lazarus, A. A., & Beutler, L. E. (1993). On technical eclecticism. *Journal of Counseling & Development, 71,* 381–385.

Lazarus, A. A., Beutler, L. E., & Norcross, J. C. (1992). The future of technical eclecticism. *Psychotherapy, 29,* 11–20.

Lazarus, A. A., & Davison, G. C. (1971). Clinical innovation in research and practice. In A. E. Bergin & S. L. Garfield (Eds.), *Handbook of Psychotherapy and Behavior Change.* New York: Wiley.

Lazarus, A. A., & Fay, A. (1982). Resistance or rationalization? A cognitive-behavioral perspective. In P. L. Wachtel (Ed.), *Resistance: psychodynamic and behavioral approaches.* New York: Plenum.

Lazarus, A. A., & Fay, A. (1984). Behavior therapy. In. T. B. Karasu (Ed.), *The psychiatric therapies.* Washington, DC: American Psychiatric Press.

Lazarus, A. A., & Fay, A. (1990). Brief psychotherapy: Tautology or oxymoron? In J. K. Zeig & S. G. Gilligan (Eds.), *Brief therapy: Myths, methods, and metaphors.* New York: Brunner/Mazel.

Lazarus, A. A., & Fay, A. (1992). *I can If I want to.* New York: Morrow.

Lazarus, A. A., & Lazarus, C. N. (1991). *Multimodal life history inventory.* Champaign, IL: Research Press.

Lazarus, A. A., Lazarus, C. N., & Fay, A. (1993). *Don't believe it for a minute! 40 toxic ideas that are driving you crazy.* San Luis Obispo, CA: Impact.

Lazarus, A. A. , & Mayne, T. J. (1990). Relaxation: Some limitations, side effects, and proposed solutions. *Psychotherapy, 27,* 261–266.

Lazarus, A. A. & Messer, S. B. (1991). Does chaos prevail? An exchange on technical eclecticism and assimilative integration. *Journal of Psychotherapy Integration, 1,* 143–158.

Lazarus, C. N. (1991). Conventional diagnostic nomenclature versus multimodal assessment. *Psychological Reports, 68,* 1363–1367.

Leiblum, S. R., & Rosen, R. C. (Eds.), 1988. *Sexual desire disorders.* New York: Guilford.

Lief, H. I. (1977). What's new in sex research? Inhibited sexual desire. *Medical Aspects of Human Sexuality, 2*(7), 94–95.

London, P. (1964). *The modes and morals of psychotherapy.* New York: Holt, Rinehart & Winston.

Masters, W. H., & Johnson, V. E. (1970). *Human sexual inadequacy.* Boston: Little, Brown.

Meichenbaum, D. (1994). *A clinical handbook/practical therapist manual for assessing and treating adults with post-traumatic stress disorder (PTSD).* Ontario, Canada: Institute Press.

Menninger, K. (1958). *Theory of psychoanalytic technique.* New York: Basic.

Messer, S. B., & Warren, C. S. (1995). *Models of brief psychodynamic therapy.* New York: Guilford.

Miller, N. E., & Dworkin, D. (1977). Critical issues in therapeutic applications of biofeedback, In G. E. Schwartz & J. Beatty (Eds.), *Biofeedback: Theory and research.* New York: Academic.

Mueser, K. T., & Glynn, S. M. (1995). *Behavioral family therapy for psychiatric disorders.* Needham Heights, MA: Allyn & Bacon.

Omer, H. (1994). *Critical interventions in psychotherapy.* New York: Norton.

Peterson, D. R. (1995). The reflective educator. *American Psychologist, 50,* 975–983.

Prochaska, J. O., & DiClemente, C. C. (1992). The transtheoretical approach. In J. C. Norcross & M. R. Goldfried (Eds.), *Handbook of psychotherapy integration.* New York: Basic.

Prochaska, J. O., Norcross, J. C., & DiClemente, C. C. (1994). *Changing for good.* New York: Avon.

Reid, W. H. (1980). *Basic intensive psychotherapy.* New York: Brunner/Mazel.

Rescorla, R. A. (1988). Pavlovian conditioning: It's not what you think it is. *American Psychologist, 43,* 151–160.

Rogers, C. R. (1957). The necessary and sufficient conditions of therapeutic personality change. *Journal of Consulting Psychology, 21,* 95–103.

Rosen, R. C., & Leiblum, S. R. (Eds.).(1995). *Case studies in sex therapy.* New York: Guilford.

Rudolph, J. A. (1985). Multimodal treatment of agoraphobia: A problem-focused approach. In A. A. Lazarus (Ed.), *Casebook of multimodal therapy.* New York: Guilford.

Safran, J. D., Crocker, P., McMain, S., & Murray, P. (1990). Therapeutic alliance rupture as a therapeutic event for empirical investigation. *Psychotherapy, 27,* 154–165.

Seligman, M. E. P. (1994). *What you can change & what you can't.* New York: Knopf.

Shapiro, F. (1995). *Eye movement desensitization and reprocessing.* New York: Guilford.

Shevrin, H., & Dickman, S. (1980).The psychological unconscious: A necessary assumption for all psychological theory? *American Psychologist, 35,* 421–434.

Sifneos, P. E. (1992). *Short-term, anxiety-provoking psychotherapy.* New York: Basic.

Small, L. (1971). *The briefer psychotherapies.* New York: Brunner/Mazel.

Staats, A. W. (1996). *Behavior and personality.* New York: Springer Publishing.

Strunk, W., & White, E. B. (1979). *The elements of style* (3rd ed.).New York: Macmillan.

Talmon, M. (1993). *Single session solutions.* New York: Addison-Wesley.

Tyrer, P. J. (1982). Anxiety states. In E. S. Paykel (Ed.), *Handbook of affective disorders.* New York: Guilford.

Watzlawick, P., Weakland, J., & Fisch, R. (1974). *Change: Principles of problem formation and problem resolution.* New York: Norton.

Wells, R. A., & Gianetti, V. J. (Eds.) (1990). *Handbook of the brief psychotherapies.* New York: Plenum.

Wilson, G. T. (1995). Empirically validated treatments as a basis for clinical practice: Problems and prospects. In S. C. Hayes, V. M. Folette, R. D., Dawes, & K. Grady (Eds.), *Scientific standards of psychological practice: Issues and recommendations.* Reno, NV: Context.

Woolfolk, R. L. (1992). Hermeneutics, social constructionism, and other items of intellectual fashion: Intimations for clinical science. *Behavior Therapy, 23,* 213–223.

Zeig, J. K., & Gilligan, S. G. (Eds.) (1990). *Brief therapy: Myths, methods, and metaphors.* New York: Brunner/Mazel.

Zilbergeld, B. (1978). *Male sexuality.* New York: Bantam.

Zilbergeld, B. (1992). *The new male sexuality.* New York: Bantam

Zilbergeld, B., & Lazarus, A. A. (1987). *Mind power.* New York: Ivy.

Name Index

Abenis-Cintron, A., 17
Ammerman, R. T., 45, 167
Anderson, T., 23, 165
Arkowitz, H., 43, 162, 165

Bach, G. R., 110, 165
Bandura, A., 39, 40, 155, 159, 162, 165
Barlow, D. H., 43, 153, 154, 162, 165
Barzun, J., 165
Beck, A. T., 90, 165
Beitman, B. D., 161, 162
Bekhterev, V. M., 38
Bemporad, J. R., 98, 165
Berenbaum, H., 6, 165
Beutler, L. E., 7, 19, 43, 155, 161, 162, 163, 165, 168, 169
Borkovec, T. D., 117, 167
Borys, D. S., 13, 165
Budman, S. H., 6, 7, 62, 165

Cannon, J. A., 6, 168
Carter, M. M., 43, 154, 162, 165
Cerny, J. A., 43, 165
Chambless, D., 45, 65, 165
Chevron, E. S., 45, 167
Clarkin, J. F., 161, 162
Consoli, A. J., 19, 165
Cooper, J. F., 6 ,165
Craighead, W. E., 26, 166
Craske, M. G., 43, 165
Crews, F., 36, 166

Crocker, P., 116, 170
Cummings, N. A., 62, 166

Davanloo, H., 7, 166
Davison, G. C., 26, 42, 43, 123, 166, 169
Dickman, S., 39, 158, 163, 170
DiClemente, C. C., 8, 116, 170
de Shazer, S., 30
Dreiblatt, I. S., 6, 166
Dryden, W., 7, 94, 95, 125, 157, 162, 166
Dworkin, D., 117, 170

Ellis, A., 31, 67, 68, 69, 102, 166
Erickson, M. H., 24

Fairburn, C. G., 45, 166
Fay, A., 11, 12, 13, 21, 64, 65, 111, 166, 169
Feyerabend, P., 35
Fisch, R., 41, 170
Frank, J. D., 161, 162
Frankl, V., 42, 166
Franks, C. M., 44, 156, 162, 166
Freud, S., 153, 163

Gabbard, G. O., 20, 166
Garfield, S. L., 161, 163
Gergen, K. J., 37, 166
Gianetti, V. J., 7, 170
Gilligan, S. G., 7, 170
Glynn, S. M., 44, 170
Goldfried, M. R., 26, 161, 163, 166

Goodkin, B., 11, 166
Gottman, J., 110, 166
Gurman, A. S., 7, 165
Gutheil, T. G., 20, 167

Hadley, S. W., 153, 163
Haley, J., 24, 167
Heide, F. J., 117, 167
Held, B. S., 37, 167
Herman, S. M., 61, 67, 105, 167
Hersen, M., 45, 167
Holdstock, T. L., 121, 168
Horney, K., 31, 167, 168
Howard, G. S., 116, 167
Howard, K. I., 7, 167
Hoyt, M. F., 6, 7, 167

Johnson, V. E., 78, 169

Karasu, T. B., 71, 72, 167
Karpel, M. A., 113, 167
Katzenbach, J. R., 22, 167
Kazdin, A. E., 44, 167
Kellermann, P. F., 22, 167
Kennedy, R., 117, 167
Kertész, R., 126
Klerman, G. L., 45, 167
Koegler, R. R., 6, 168
Kopp, R. R., 113, 168
Kopta, S. M., 7, 167, 168
Krause, M. S., 7, 167
Kuhn, T., 35
Kwee, M. G. T., 44, 120, 121, 125, 168

Landes, A. A., 61, 168
Lambert, M. J., 153, 163, 168
Lazarus, A. A., 3, 5, 11–14, 18, 19, 26, 32,
    37, 42–44, 64, 65, 68, 72, 82, 94, 98,
    100, 101, 108, 110, 117, 120, 123,
    153–156, 163, 166, 168, 169, 170
Lazarus, C. N., 3, 32, 61, 65, 82, 90, 94, 117,
    125, 145, 154, 163, 169
Leiblum, S. R., 2, 78, 88, 169, 170
Lief, H. I., 78, 169
London, P., 42, 71, 169
Lowry, J. L., 7, 168

Masters, W. H., 78, 169
Mayne, T. J., 118, 169
McMain, S., 116, 170
Meichenbaum, D., 8, 169
Messer, S. B., 37, 71, 156, 163, 169
Menninger, K., 77, 169
Miller, N. E., 117, 170
Moreno, Z., 22
Mueser, K. T., 44, 170
Murray, P., 116, 170
Myers, P., 116, 167

Nadelson, C., 20, 166
Nance, D. W., 116, 167
Newman, C. F., 161, 163
Norcross, J. C., 8, 43, 155, 161, 163, 169, 170
Nuland, S. B., 16, 161, 163

Omer, H., 62, 170
Orlinski, D. E., 7, 167
Osgood, C., 158, 163

Palmer, S., 125
Paul, G. L., 162, 163
Peterson, D. R., 20, 170
Prochaska, J. O., 8, 116, 170

Reid, W. H., 39, 170
Rescorla, R. A., 38, 170
Rhoads, J. M., 156, 163
Rogers, C. R., 11, 170
Rosen, R. C., 2, 78, 88, 169, 170
Rounsaville, B. J., 45, 147
Rudolph, J. A., 61, 170

Safran, J. D., 116, 170
Sayama, M., 62, 166
Scaturo, D. J., 158, 159, 163
Seligman, M. E. P., 45, 170
Shapiro, F., 44, 170
Shevrin, H., 39, 158, 163, 170
Sifneos, P. E., 7, 170
Small, J., 7, 170
Staats, A. W., 44, 170
Strunk, W., 14, 15, 170
Strupp, H. H., 153, 163

Talmon, M., 76, 170
Turovsky, J., 43, 154, 162, 165
Tyrer, P. J., 41, 170

Wachtel, P. L., 156, 163
Watzlawick, P., 41, 170
Warren, C. S., 72, 169
Weakland, J., 41, 170
Weatherly, D., 6, 166
Weissman, M. M., 45, 167

Wells, R. A., 7, 170
White, E. B., 14, 15, 170
Williams, R. E., 20, 165
Wilson, G. T., 44, 170
Wolpe, J., 154, 163
Woolfolk, R. L., 37, 170
Wyden, P., 110, 165

Zeig, J. K., 7, 170
Zilbergeld, B., 26, 84, 170

Subject Index

Advising clients, 71–73
Affect, 91
  gaining access through bridging, 48–50
Alcoholism, 19
Alcohol cravings, 58–59
American Psychologist (journal), 20
Analogies and metaphors, 112–113
Assertion vs. aggression, 58
Associations and relations among events, 38
Association for Advancement of Behavior Therapy, 26
Authentic chameleons, 18

Badgering a client, 47, 48
BASIC I.D.:
  assessment, 2
  defined, 1
  in perspective, 3, 26–30
  ripple effect, 5
  second-order assessments, 57–59
Behavior Therapy and Beyond (Lazarus), 26
Bespoke therapy, 16
Bibliotherapy, 64, 65
Biological factors, 3, 4, 9, 27–28, 30, 32, 80, 93, 104
Boundaries, 12–13, 20–24
Breadth vs. depth, 11, 19
Bridging, 48–52
Brief Rational Emotive Behavior Therapy (Dryden), 94

Brief Therapy and Managed Care (Hoyt), 7
Brief Therapy: Myths, Methods, and Metaphors (Zeig & Gilligan), 7
Brief therapy:
  definition, 6
  selection criteria, 7, 8
  temporal considerations, 6, 7
Broad-spectrum behavior therapy, 123

Centre for Multimodal Therapy (London), 125
Client-therapist relationship, 11–12
Clinical Behavior Therapy (Goldfried & Davison), 26
Common factors approach, 161
Constructs, seven, 38–42
Couples therapy, 101–114
  amicable divorces, 113–114
  analogies and metaphors, 112–113
  double (technique of), 109–110
  individual vs. dyadic, 102, 104
  "magic ratio", 110
  saying "no!" 111–112
  seven basic ground rules, 101–102
  time-limited intercommunication, 107–108
  triple increase technique, 102–104

Defensive reactions, 39–40
Double (technique of), 109–110
DSM-IV, 88, 89, 90

Dysthymic disorder, 88–90
  application, 93–94
  predominantly cognitive case, 94–98
  treatment, 90–93

Egoless state of being, 69, 70
Eight issues to be ruled out, 9
Entry points into therapy, 4
Experimentally validated procedures, 44, 45

"Firing orders," 52–56
Forgotten memory, 56
Follow-ups, 4, 123
Forms of Brief Therapy (Budman), 7
Formula for brief but comprehensive psychotherapy, 4, 5
Four principles of multimodal therapy, 5

Generalization, 12

Handbook on the Brief Psychotherapies (Wells & Gianetti), 7
Handbook of Prescriptive Treatments for Adults (Hersen & Ammerman), 45
Human Sexual Inadequacy (Masters & Johnson), 78
Humor, 120–121

I Can If I Want To (Lazarus & Fay), 64
Imagery example, 50–52
Inhibited sexual desire:
  issues in disorders, 79–81
  case presentation, 81–88
Initial interviews, twelve issues to be addressed, 10
Integration, 159–161
Internet, 125
Irrational thinking, common patterns, 95

Love and caring, 102
Low frustration tolerance, 67

Main points and tactics (summarized), 124
Male Sexuality (Zilbergeld), 84
Marital Myths (Lazarus), 87
Marital Satisfaction Questionnaire, 105–107, 149–150

Matching:
  Don (elitist), 18
  Maria (Hispanic girl), 17
Metacommunications, 40–41
Metaphor Therapy (Kopp), 113
Modality Profiles, 32, 84, 89
Modeling and imitation, 39
Multimodal Behavior Therapy (Lazarus), 46
Multimodal Life History Inventory, 3, 32, 82, 83, 94, 105, 153
  not applied, 117
Multimodal therapy:
  in Argentina, 125–126
  in England, 125
  in Netherlands, 125
  vs. Rational-Emotive Behavior Therapy (REBT), 68
Myths that undermine brief therapy, 10–13

Noncompliance and "resistance," 13
Nonconscious processes, 39

Observations, 36
Occam's razor, 37

Paradoxical remarks, 97
Parsimony, principle of, 37
Pets (as therapy), 73–74
Physical features, 74–77
Private events, 40

Range of alternatives (ROAs), 97–98
Readiness for change, 116–117
REBT (Ellis), 26, 67–70
  differences with multimodal therapy (MMT), 68
Referrals, 66, 67
Relationship styles, 14
Relaxation-induced anxiety, 117
Resistance (*see* Noncompliance)
Response couplets, 120
Ritalin, 117

Second-order BASIC I.D., 57–59
Selection criteria, 7–8
Sensory reactions, 49
Sexual Desire Disorders (Leiblum & Rosen), 88

Spirituality, 42
Structural Profiles, 59–61
Structural Profile Inventory (SPI), 61, 143–144
  expanded, 61, 105, 145–148
  predicting outcomes, 67
Supervision group, 125
Symptom substitution, 123

Take no crap (TNC) outlook, 117
Technical eclecticism, 42–45, 108–110, 151–162
Temporal factors, 30–32
The New Male Sexuality (Zilbergeld), 84
Theories, 35, 36
  and observations, 36–38
Theory of Psychoanalytic Technique (Menninger), 77
Thresholds, 41–42

Time-limited intercommunication, 107–108
Time-tripping imagery, 85–86, 98–100
Time wasters:
  analyzing the "transference," 116
  failing to take action, 118–121
  ignoring readiness for change, 116–117
  needless delving into the past, 115–116
  panacea pundits, 117–118
  waiting for the client to draw conclusions, 121–122
Tracking, 52–56
Treatments of choice, 153–154

Unconditional self-acceptance, 67
Unimodal and multimodal perspectives, 19
Using fax, e-mail, telephone, and letters, 63

World Wide Web, 125

Springer Publishing Company

The Practice of Rational Emotive Behavior Therapy
Second Edition
Albert Ellis, PhD, and Windy Dryden, PhD

This volume systematically reviews the practice of Rational Emotive Behavior Therapy and shows how it can be used by therapists in a variety of clinical settings. The book begins with an explanation of REBT as a general treatment model. It then addresses different treatment modalities, including individual, couple, family, and sex therapy.

The new edition modernizes the pioneering theories of Albert Ellis and contains a complete updating of references over the past ten years. The authors have added new information on teaching the principles of unconditional self-acceptance in a structured, group setting. With extensive use of actual case examples to illustrate each of the different settings, this volume will appeal to clinical and counseling psychologists as well as any other helping professionals involved in therapy.

Contents:

The General Theory of REBT • The Basic Practice of REBT • A Case Illustration of the Basic Practice of REBT: The Case of Jane • Individual Therapy • Couples Therapy • Family Therapy • Group Therapy • Rational Emotive Behavior Marathons and Intensives • Teaching the Principles of Unconditioned Self-Acceptance in a Structured Group Setting • The Rational Emotive Behavioral Approach to Sex Therapy • The Use of Hypnosis with REBT • How to Maintain and Enhance Your Rational Emotive Behavior Therapy Gains

1997   280pp   0-8261-5471-9   hardcover

536 Broadway, New York, NY 10012-3955 • (212) 431-4370 • Fax (212) 941-7842